How the Witchcraft Spirit Operates & the Anointing that Destroys It

By

Prophetess Mary J. Ogenaarekhua

Endorsement

Dedication

As with all my books, I dedicate this book to my heavenly Father, my Lord Jesus Christ and my Lord the Holy Spirit. LORD God, You gave me the words to write in this book and I thank You for it because without Your teachings, I will not have anything to write. I thank You for teaching me about how the witchcraft spirit operates and how to destroy it. Thanks also for giving me the grace to write what You taught me as it is written in **Psalm 68:11**:

> *"The Lord gave the word: great was the company of those that published it."*

LORD God, may this book bring You much glory and may You use it to set many free from the wickedness of the witchcraft spirit.

I also dedicate this book to all those who have been in battle with the witchcraft spirit and have been seeking deliverance from the Lord. I hope that this book is a major tool in your hand to walk in victory over this wicked spirit.

How the Witchcraft Spirit Operates & the Anointing that Destroys It

Unless otherwise indicated, all scriptures are quoted from the King James Version of the Bible.

Published by: **To His Glory Publishing Company, Inc.**
463 Dogwood Drive, NW
Lilburn, GA 30047
(770) 458-7947
www.tohisglorypublishing.com

This Book is available at:
Amazon.com, BarnesandNoble.com, Booksamillion.com, UK, EU, Canada, Australia, etc.

Also, see the Order Form at the back of this book or call/ email below to order this book.

(770) 458-7947
www.tohisglorypublishing.com
Email: tohisglorypublishing@yahoo.com

ISBN: 978-1-942724-02-5

Table of Contents

Preface 13
Acknowledgments 15

Chapter 1:
What is the Witchcraft Spirit 17
Common Mistakes Concerning the Witchcraft Spirit 17
Misuse of the Practice of Identifying a Witch or a Wizard ...18
Definition of a Witch and a Wizard 19
Definition of Witchcraft 19
How God Feels about the Practice of Witchcraft 20

Chapter 2:
The Kings of Israel and the Practice of Witchcraft 23
King Saul's Involvement in the Witchcraft Practice 23
King Manasseh's Involvement in Witchcraft Practice 27

Chapter 3:
Tools of the Witchcraft Spirit 31
Use of Soothsaying or Predictions 31
Activities of Familiar Spirits 32
The End Does Not Justify the Means 33
How People Get Involved in Witchcraft through Idolatry 36
The Devil's Attempt to Recruit Me into Idolatry 37

Chapter 4:
Satanic Covens and the Satanic Church 39
Use of Blood in Human and Animal Sacrifices 39
Use of Sexual Abuse 40
Saying of 'Black Mass' 40
Strong Hatred of the God of the Bible and Christians 41
Use of Black Magic and White Magic 41
Casting of Spells 42
Channeling of Thoughts 43
Engage in Evil Meditation 44

Chapter 5:

The West African Type of Witchcraft 49
The Power of the 'Born Again' Christian 49
The West African Definition of a Witch 49
How People Become Witches or Wizards...........................51
The Witches' Call to Flight at Night 52
The Toll of the Nightly Flights on the Human Body 53
Being Pressed by Witches on Your Bed 57
The Request to Kill 58

Chapter 6:

Ways Witchcraft Spirit Oppress Its Victims 61
No Assignment against 'Born Again' Christians 61
Witches and Wizards that Peep and Mutter 62
Eavesdropping Spirits 64
Hindrances by the Witchcraft Spirit 69
Covenants with the Witchcraft Spirit or Familiar Spirits 69
Healing 'Powers' of Witchdoctors 75
The Aid of Familiar Spirits in Modern Society 76
Familiar Spirits Appearing in Visions and Dreams 77
My Victory over the Witchcraft Spirit of 'Mind Control' 78

Chapter 7:

The Voodoo Type of Witchcraft 81
What is Voodoo? 81
The Origin of Voodoo 81
The Goal of Voodoo Practitioners 82
The Role of the Serpent in Voodoo Practice 84
Voodoo Rituals 86
The Wicked Activities of the Voodoo Priests and Priestesses ...87
'Blanking Out' Someone's Mind 87
Use of Sorcery and Divination 89
The Difference between West African Witchcraft and Voodoo 90

Chapter 8:

Santeria as a Form of Witchcraft 93
Origin of Santeria 93

The Slaves' Attempts to Deceive Their Masters 93
The Essence of Santeria 94
Santeria's Influence in Cuba 94
Santeria's Influence in the United States 95
The Quest for Power and Knowledge 95
The Witchcraft Prayer of 'Binding People to God's Will' 97

Chapter 9:
New Age Movement and Other Witchcraft Organizations 99
The Composition of the New Age Doctrine 99
Satanic Influence in the New Age Doctrine 99
The Hippie Influence on New Age 100
A Word about Yoga 101

Chapter 10:
Religions with Satanic and Witchcraft Roots 103
Witchcraft Roots of Pagan Religions 103
Pagan Religions of Europe 104
Impact of the Pagan Religions of Egypt 105
The Impact of Roman Religion 111
The Impact of Greek Idolatry and Mythology 112
Zeus and Europa's Influence on Europe and the World 112
The Greek Pythia's Influences on the World 114
The Pythian Games as the Origin of the Olympic Games 115
The Impact of the Greek Mindset on the World through Education 116
Pagan Religions Outlined in the Bible 118

Chapter 11:
Characteristics of the Different Types of Witchcraft 121
Jesus Is the Light of the World 121
Children of Light & Children of Darkness 122
Common Denominator in Secret Societies 124
Common Denominator among Witches 125
Common Denominator among Mediums 126
The Lady 'Performing Cure' with Demonic Powers 127

Chapter 12:

Things that Invite the Witchcraft Spirit 131
Walking in Rebellion 131
Walking in Envy and Jealousy 131
Walking in Covetousness 132
Walking in Hatred and Resentment 133
Walking in Unforgiveness 134
Seeking Revenge and Retaliation 134
Walking in Offense and Anger 135
The Holy Spirit Activates Your Spirit to Fight Witches at Night 137
A Vision of How Our Spirit Fights 138

Chapter 13:

How to Overcome the Witchcraft Spirit 139
Avoid Rebellion against God: Be 'Born Again' 139
Be Grounded in the Word of God 140
Repent of Ancestral or Generational Witchcraft Covenants 142
Have an Active Prayer and Fasting Life 143
Affirm Your New Bloodline and Heritage in Christ 144
Use the Name of Jesus 145
Avoid the Works of the Flesh 147
Avoid Evil Gifts 148
Avoid Playful Activities that are Evil 148

Conclusion 151
Prayer to Make Jesus the Lord of Your Life.................152

Appendix A 153
Appendix B 159
Glossary of Definitions 163
About the Author 167
Bibliography 175

Preface

This book is intended to give the reader a deep understanding of how the witchcraft spirit operates. In it, you will learn about the different types of witchcraft in various parts of the world, their activities and their common denominators. You will also learn about the tools of the witchcraft spirit, what attracts and what repels it as well as how to identify a witchcraft assignment. It will also open your eyes to know why some witches are more powerful than others and how to defeat them all. Due to today's reality of living in a global community, a lot of the witchcraft activities that were once confined to certain continents are now found in various countries all over the world. As Christians, we need to be equipped on how to identify and overcome them.

My goal is to help all those who read this book to deal with the regional and global witchcraft activities that are operating in their lives, families, workplaces, cities, states and countries. What you learn in this book will prepare you to deal with all types of witchcraft activities that you may encounter in any part of the world that you choose to visit or minister in. You will be able to deal with this 'strongman' and its influences without fear of retaliation. Just be brave and as the Lord said, "fear not."

—Prophetess Mary J. Ogenaarekhua

Acknowledgements

Heavenly Father, I acknowledge the great deliverance that You have given me over the witchcraft spirit and for fulfilling Your Word to me through Your Son, my Lord Jesus Christ that:

"If the Son therefore shall make you free, ye shall be free indeed" (John 8:36).

Thank You Lord that I am truly free indeed. Thank You for using me to set many free with Your Word and Your Spirit.

As always, thank you Lynne Garbinsky for the many hours that you spent in formatting, laying out and proofreading this book. You are a steadfast soldier and may the Lord bless you beyond your imagination.

I also thank all the people that have shared their personal warfare with the witchcraft spirit with me. It is my hope that by the help of the Holy Spirit and in the name of the Lord Jesus, this book will bring you the much desired deliverance that you have been praying for. May the Lord bless you with total victory as you read this book.

Chapter 1
What is the Witchcraft Spirit

Common Mistakes Concerning the Witchcraft Spirit

A lot of times, people tell me that **rebellion, stubbornness** and certain **other demonic activities** are witchcraft. They say this because the **Prophet Samuel** rebuked King Saul after he **disobeyed** the Lord's instructions (rebellion) to destroy all the Amalekites and their animals. Instead, King Saul saved the Amalekite King and some of the animals. His excuse was that he saved the animals so that he can offer them as sacrifices to God. In response, the Prophet Samuel said the following in **1 Samuel 15:22-23** and he likened rebellion to the sin of witchcraft:

> "...Hath the LORD as great delight in burnt offerings and sacrifices, as in <u>**obeying** the voice of the LORD?</u> <u>Behold, to obey is better than sacrifice, and to hearken than the fat of rams.</u> 23 **For rebellion is as the sin of witchcraft, and stubbornness is as iniquity and idolatry...**"

As a result of this rebuke by the Prophet Samuel, **many people now have a limited definition of witchcraft. They tend to only associate the witchcraft spirit with just rebellion, stubbornness, envy, jealousy, etc.** The witchcraft spirit is much deeper and more serious than just rebellion, stubbornness and acts of iniquity. **An important observation from the above scripture is that to be as something is not being the real thing itself.** For example, the devil is referred to as acting "as a roaring lion" in **1 Peter 5:8:**

> "Be sober, be vigilant; because your adversary the devil, **as a roaring lion**, walketh about, seeking whom he may devour."

We all know that <u>the devil is not a true lion</u> because the **Real Lion is from the Tribe of Judah** which is **the Lord**

Jesus Christ. The devil likes to portray himself as a lion in order to lie and to deceive people but the truth is that he is not the real LION. **Therefore, to be as witchcraft is not the same as witchcraft itself.**

Misuse of the Practice of Identifying a Witch or a Wizard

When the Bible talks about witchcraft, it is talking about **witches and wizards who use familiar spirits** to do different things. Some of them supposedly do 'good things' but we know that no good can come from the devil. Therefore, to call a person a witch, you have to make sure that you are talking about **a person that uses familiar spirits**. Unfortunately, when you read the history of Western nations during the era of the 'Spanish Inquisition' (the time that they were burning people at the stakes), they were not persecuting true witches and wizards. Rather, a lot of people saw it as a means of getting rid of their political or spiritual adversaries. In other words, identifying a person as a witch became a tool to eliminate one's enemies. **They used little children to accuse many innocent people of being witches; usually, it was someone who stood up against the misuse of 'absolute power' by the King, the Church or influential members of society.**

At this time in human history, kings, queens, popes and lawmakers viewed themselves as very important and with tremendous influence in societies that they placed themselves above the law. As a result, they would trump up the charges of being a witch or wizard against anyone that they wanted to get rid of. Hence we have very many examples of this type of abuse of power with an unprecedented burning of innocent people at the stakes in the 16th and 17th centuries. The very prominent one in Europe is that of Joan of Arc who was condemned to death and burnt at the stakes in 1431 and exonerated of the charges in 1456. In the United States, there are the 'Salem Witch Hunts' in colonial Massachusetts.

We are to learn from their wickedness and from their mistakes by being properly informed about what witchcraft is and what it is not. **We cannot go around accusing innocent people of being what they are not, neither can we afford to be ignorant when we are truly confronted with witches and their witchcraft activities.**

Definition of a Witch and a Wizard

A **witch** is a **woman** that is credited with having super-natural powers and who practices magic or witchcraft with the aids of devils or familiar spirits. A **wizard** is a **man** who performs magic or witchcraft with the aids of familiar spirits; it is the masculine form of a witch. I know that today, many people refer to **someone who is particularly skillful at a certain activity as a wizard** but this latter use of the word wizard is not what I am referring to in this book. Rather, I am writing about the men and women who use the aids of familiar spirits to practice demonic activities.

When a man operates with a witchcraft spirit, we call him a wizard and when a woman is doing the same, she is called a witch. In time past, **Wicca** was the term used for a male wizard while **Wicce** was used for a female witch. Both witches and wizards interact with the spirit of death or practice necromancy. In other words, they talk to familiar spirits pretending to be the spirits of those who have died and gone on. **Witchcraft and its practice is not a superstitious belief as some people like to think in Western nations.** It is a serious sin before God. The bottom line is that God hates sin and yes, there are different categories of sins but the final destination is the same for all types of sins—hell!

Definition of Witchcraft

In the dictionary, **witchcraft** is defined as:

1. The use of supernatural powers
2. Communication with the devil or with a familiar spirit
3. A fascination with the demonic
4. Use of magic, sorcery, divination, soothsaying

We can see from this definition that someone who is stubborn but does not necessarily deal with familiar spirits is not into witchcraft. Also, someone can be stubborn without possessing any supernatural powers and without dabbling in anything demonic. The traits of stubbornness and rebellion do not make someone a witch or a wizard but what the Prophet Samuel wanted King Saul to know was that disobedience or rebellion is as grievous to God as the sin of witchcraft. **The reason is because <u>a sin is a sin</u> and <u>all sins lead to death</u>; spiritual death or eternal separation from God** —Ezekiel 18:4:

> "Behold, all souls are mine; as the soul of the father, so also the soul of the son is mine: **the soul that sinneth, it shall die.**"

A lot of people believe that the practice of witchcraft exists only in Africa and some other developing countries and they do not believe that true witchcraft exists in societies such as the United States and other developed countries. **This is a lie from the pit of hell because the witchcraft spirit disguises itself in societies depending on the platform it is given.** Therefore, do not let anyone tell you that warring against the witchcraft spirit is a figment of your imagination because God Himself acknowledges that it exists.

How God Feels about the Practice of Witchcraft

There are scriptures that God meant to help us understand that the practice of witchcraft is not something that Christians made up or something that only exists in primitive societies. During the time of the law, God did not want the children of Israel to have any room for witchcraft in the entire nation. Therefore, He gave them a law concerning it as we can see in **Deuteronomy 18:9-14:**

> "When thou art come into the land which the LORD thy God giveth thee, thou shalt not learn to do after the abominations of those nations. *10* **There shall not be found among you any one that maketh his son or**

**his daughter to pass through the fire, or that useth
divination, or an observer of times, or an enchanter,
or <u>a witch</u>,**

11 **Or a charmer, or a consulter with familiar
spirits, or a wizard, or a necromancer.** *12* <u>For all
that do these things are an abomination unto the
LORD</u>: and because of these abominations the
LORD thy God doth drive them out from before
thee. *13* Thou shalt be perfect with the LORD
thy God. *14* **For these nations, which thou shalt
possess, hearkened unto observers of times, and
unto diviners: but as for thee, the LORD thy God
hath not suffered thee so to do.**"

As we can see from the scripture above, the tools used by
those practicing witchcraft are **divination, human sacrifice**
(burning children in the fire), **enchantment, charms, familiar
spirits, observation of times, necromancy** or **'talking with
the dead'**, etc. <u>The practice of witchcraft was one of the
primary reasons why God could freely remove the nations
that had occupied the land that He brought the children
of Israel into</u>. They became abominable in the sight of God
because of their many witchcraft practices and because
their whole lifestyles were based on these evil practices.
God rejected them and removed them from His land.

**God owns the earth and He has a right to remove
those who reject Him and choose to worship some other
god or gods from His land.** God regards these practices as
abominations —an abomination is something that makes
God to look away and cover His eyes because He does not
behold sin. **As a result, when a person begins to dabble in
witchcraft, he or she becomes abominable in the sight of
God.** He told us in **Leviticus 19:31** not to defile ourselves with
those who practice witchcraft:

**"Regard not them that have familiar spirits, neither
seek after wizards,** <u>to be defiled by them</u>: I am the
LORD your God."

Christian Definition of Witchcraft

As Christians, we define witchcraft as the power of a person to influence or to harm another person with the aid of familiar spirits using occultic, natural or supernatural means. This is why God hates witchcraft and He showed us in scriptures just how much He hates it by pronouncing a death sentence on all witches (male or female). His judgment on witchcraft in **Exodus 22:18** is also a biblical acknowledgment that witchcraft is real:

> **"Thou shalt not suffer a witch to live."**

And also in **Leviticus 20:6-8**:

> **"And the soul that turneth after such as have familiar spirits, and after wizards, to go a whoring after them, I will even set my face against that soul, and will cut him off from among his people.** 7 Sanctify yourselves therefore, and be ye holy: for I am the LORD your God. 8 And ye shall keep my statutes, and do them: I am the LORD which sanctify you."

In other words, when someone is identified as a witch or as one who conjures up familiar spirits or uses familiar spirits to do magic and other demonic things, the children of Israel were to kill that person publicly; they were not to suffer the person to live. **Just because Christians are now under GRACE does not mean that God now permits the practice of witchcraft but rather that those who practice it will turn from it and receive His salvation in Christ.** If they refuse, they leave God no choice but to judge and send them to hell in the end. God's hatred for witchcraft is forever. He again emphasized His judgment on the practice of witchcraft in **Leviticus 20:27**:

> **"A man also or woman that hath a familiar spirit, or that is a wizard, shall surely be put to death:** they shall stone them with stones: their blood shall be upon them."

Chapter 2
The Kings of Israel and the Practice of Witchcraft

King Saul's Involvement in the Witchcraft Practice

Saul was Israel's very first king and he was handpicked by God Himself. He initially carried out God's commandment not "to suffer a witch to live" by destroying all the witches that were in Israel. As his kingdom began to be established, King Saul chose to disobey the instructions from God and the Prophet Samuel judged and stripped the kingdom from him. King Saul's involvement in witchcraft began when the Philistines came to war against him and he tried to get the Word of the Lord concerning the outcome of the battle but God refused to talk to him because of his disobedience to His instructions.

Since he could not get the Word of the Lord concerning the battle, King Saul decided to go against the Word of God concerning the practice of witchcraft by consulting a witch. He totally ignored the fact that when he had a zeal for the Lord, he destroyed witches and their institution of witchcraft in all of Israel. King Saul commanded his servants to seek out a witch for him to consult and they found a witch in Endor that he could go to as recorded in **1 Samuel 28:7-10.** He disguised himself and went to visit the witch who can use familiar spirits to divine for him:

> "Then said Saul unto his servants, **Seek me a woman that hath a familiar spirit, that I may go to her, and enquire of her.** And his servants said to him, Behold, there is a woman that hath a familiar spirit at Endor.
> 8 **And Saul disguised himself, and put on other raiment, and he went, and two men with him, and they came to the woman by night: and he said, I pray thee, divine unto me by the familiar spirit, and bring me him up, whom I shall name unto thee.**

9 **And the woman said unto him, Behold, thou knowest what Saul hath done, how he hath cut off those that have familiar spirits, and the wizards, out of the land: wherefore then layest thou a snare for my life, to cause me to die?** *10* And Saul sware to her by the LORD, saying, As the LORD liveth, there shall no punishment happen to thee for this thing."

Before entertaining King Saul's request, we can see that even the witch was abiding by King Saul's law against the practice of witchcraft. Therefore, King Saul swore by the name of the Lord to the witch that he would not put her to death according to his own law before he requested the witch to bring up the Prophet Samuel. Can you imagine, King Saul swearing with the name of the Lord to a witch that uses familiar spirits?

In King Saul's encounter with this witch at Endor, we are going to see familiar spirits adapt themselves to a person's beliefs. In this case, King Saul believed that the late Prophet Samuel can rise from the dead and speak to him so, the familiar spirit in the witch was more than willing to oblige him as we see in **1 Samuel 28:11-20:**

"Then said the woman, **Whom shall I bring up unto thee? And he said, Bring me up Samuel.** *12* <u>And when the woman saw Samuel, she cried with a loud voice: and the woman spake to Saul, saying, Why hast thou deceived me? for thou art Saul</u> *(the familiar spirit blew Saul's cover).* *13* <u>And the king said unto her, Be not afraid: for what sawest thou? And the woman said unto Saul,</u> **I saw gods ascending out of the earth**.

14 And he said unto her, **What form is he of**? *(King Saul immediately assumed that it was Samuel and the spirit adapted to his belief)* <u>And she said, An old man cometh up; and he is covered with a mantle.</u> **And Saul perceived that it was Samuel, and he stooped with his face to**

the ground, and bowed himself. 15 And Samuel *(the familiar spirit is now talking)* said to Saul, Why hast thou disquieted me, to bring me up? **And Saul answered, I am sore distressed; for the Philistines make war against me, and God is departed from me, and answereth me no more, neither by prophets, nor by dreams: therefore I have called thee, that thou mayest make known unto me what I shall do**.

16 Then said Samuel *(familiar spirit)*, Wherefore then dost thou ask of me, seeing the LORD is departed from thee, and is become thine enemy? 17 And the LORD hath done to him, as he spake by me: for the LORD hath rent the kingdom out of thine hand, and given it to thy neighbour, even to David: 18 Because thou obeyedst not the voice of the LORD, nor executedst his fierce wrath upon Amalek, therefore hath the LORD done this thing unto thee this day *(This knowledge is in the public domain spiritually; every spirit knows things that happen publicly)*.

19 <u>Moreover the LORD will also deliver Israel with thee into the hand of the Philistines: and tomorrow shalt thou and thy sons be with me</u>: *(Saul accepts his destruction in a false prophesy)* the LORD also shall deliver the host of Israel into the hand of the Philistines. 20 Then Saul fell straightway all along on the earth, and was sore afraid, because of the words of Samuel: and there was no strength in him; for he had eaten no bread all the day, nor all the night."

When you analyze this conversation that King Saul had with this witch, you will see that he requested the witch **to bring up the late Prophet Samuel** for him but the witch said to King Saul, **"I <u>saw gods</u> coming out of the earth."** She spoke in <u>past tense</u> and in a <u>plural form</u> by saying, **"I saw gods"** but Saul responded in a <u>singular form</u> and in <u>present tense</u> by asking,

"**What form is <u>he</u> of**?" <u>Therefore, it was King Saul who drew his own conclusion concerning who he perceived the "**gods**"</u> to be! **Once King Saul drew his own conclusion, the spirit adapted itself to his tailor-made request as it proceeded to talk to him.**

In other words, the witch went from "<u>seeing gods coming out of the earth</u>" to "<u>seeing an old man covered with a mantel</u>" because of King Saul's **perception** that the "gods" were the late Prophet Samuel. **You should notice that she did not say that she saw gods coming out of heaven but out of the earth because she cannot see into what God is doing in heaven.** She cannot go into heaven to bring the late Prophet Samuel back through divination. The scriptures clearly told us in **Hebrews 9:27** that a person only lives once. Nobody get to come back again or come back to communicate with the living after they have died:

> "And as **it is appointed unto men once to die, but after this the judgment.**"

Always remember that only God is All-knowing; the devil cannot bring back a dead person but only a familiar spirit that will pretend to be the dead person that you are looking for. Also, he cannot tell you what God is planning because he cannot read God's mind. He can only tell you about his own plans against you and then try to blame it on another person. The spirit that spoke to King Saul never claimed to be the late prophet Samuel until King Saul called him Samuel; this is how the devil operates. He gives you enough for you to draw the wrong conclusion so that he can stand before God and say, "I never made them do anything, I just placed things before them and they make their own choices."

This is what he did to Eve in the Garden of Eden and his response is usually like this, "I just showed her the fruit but she picked and ate it all by herself." In the case of King Saul, his wrong perception of the familiar spirit made him to stoop with his face to the ground and bowed himself to the devil. **Meaning that King Saul was not aware that he was worshipping a familiar spirit when he bowed to the so-called 'Samuel' who was nothing but a familiar spirit!** You cannot fall any lower than this into idolatry and witchcraft because since this familiar spirit had his ears, he began to tell him the devil's plan to kill him and his sons.

In most cases when people lend their ears to the devil through witchcraft and its idolatry, familiar spirits begin to guide them instead of the Holy Spirit. **As we have just seen in the case of King Saul, the so-called 'Samuel' who began to talk to him, gave him a destructive prophecy and King Saul ignorantly received it.** In short, King Saul received his own destruction from the hand of the evil spirit that he bowed to. The sad part of the story was that he went of his own free will and with his own two feet to consult the familiar spirit. At the end, all that the spirit did for him was to get him to accept the devil's plans to kill him and his sons.

King Manasseh's Involvement in Witchcraft Practice

Manasseh the son of King Hezekiah did much evil in the sight of God because of his involvement in witchcraft activities. Some writers have said that if God had not healed King Hezekiah after he prayed to the Lord when he was sick, Manasseh would not have been born and Israel would have been spared a lot of anguish but we know that God is perfect and He is merciful to all who call on Him. He is a good God. As written in **2 Kings 20:1-7**, King Hezekiah became sick and prayed to God and God used the Prophet Isaiah to heal him and He added 15 years to his life:

> "**In those days was Hezekiah sick unto death.** And the prophet Isaiah the son of Amoz came to him, and said unto him, **Thus saith the LORD, Set thine house in order; for thou shalt die, and not live.** 2 Then he turned his face to the wall, and prayed unto the

LORD, saying, 3 I beseech thee, O LORD, remember now how I have walked before thee in truth and with a perfect heart, and have done that which is good in thy sight. **And Hezekiah wept sore.** 4 And it came to pass, afore Isaiah was gone out into the middle court, that the word of the LORD came to him, saying,

5 Turn again, and tell Hezekiah the captain of my people, **Thus saith the LORD, the God of David thy father, I have heard thy prayer, I have seen thy tears: behold, I will heal thee: on the third day thou shalt go up unto the house of the LORD.** 6 <u>**And I will add unto thy days fifteen years**</u>; and I will deliver thee and this city out of the hand of the king of Assyria; and I will defend this city for mine own sake, and for my servant David's sake. 7 And Isaiah said, Take a lump of figs. And they took and laid it on the boil, and he recovered."

When King Hezekiah died, Manasseh, his son became king but Manasseh followed in the ways of the very ungodly King Jeroboam. **God regarded King Jeroboam as Israel's worst king before King Manasseh because he institutionalized the worship of idols in Israel.** The biblical account of King Jeroboam's story is that in the days of King Rehoboam, Solomon's son, God divided the twelve tribes of Israel. God called Jeroboam from Egypt to be ruler over 10 tribes and He left the house of David with Judah and the tribe of Benjamin. As I wrote in detail in my book titled, *How the Jezebel Spirit Operates and the Anointing that Destroys Her, Chapter 13*:

> "…The problem was that w**hen Jeroboam became King, he set up idol worship in Bethel in order to keep the people from returning to the house of David when they go to the Temple in Jerusalem to worship God.** As a result, Bethel became the idol worship center and the people went there to worship idols instead of worshipping God at the Temple in Jerusalem…"

In other words, in Bethel, King Jeroboam setup the idol worship of the golden calves that he learned in Egypt. He convinced the people that they did not have to go to the Temple in Jerusalem to worship because the worship of the golden calves in Bethel was as good as the worship of God at the Temple in Jerusalem. By this action, King Jeroboam sold the 10 tribes of Israel into idolatry except for a few people that were still zealous for the God of Israel. **To God, Jeroboam's actions of empowering people to abandon worshiping Him and to turn to idol worship was one of the most serious sins ever committed by a king in Israel.** For this sin, God judged and destroyed the house of Jeroboam without leaving him any posterity.

When the kingdom now came over to Manasseh, he favored the ways of the late King Jeroboam. During his reign, King Manasseh elevated idol worship to a higher level. Not only did he glorify idol worship in Bethel, he also **sacrificed** (caused to pass through the fire) some of his children to the god of fire called Molech! **As if these things were not bad enough, he brought idol worship into the house of the Lord (the Jerusalem Temple); into the very Temple that Solomon built for the glory of God as stated in 2 Chronicles 33:5-10:**

> "**And he** (*Manasseh*) **built altars for all the host of heaven in the two courts of the house of the LORD.** 6 **And he caused his children to pass through the fire** (*sacrificed some of his children to the god of fire, molech*) in the valley of the son of Hinnom: **also he observed times**, and **used enchantments**, and **used witchcraft**, and **dealt with a familiar spirit**, and **with wizards**: he wrought much evil in the sight of the LORD, to provoke him to anger.
>
> 7 And **he set a carved image, the idol which he had made, in the house of God**, of which God had said to David and to Solomon his son, In this house, and in Jerusalem, which I have chosen before all the tribes of

Israel, will I put my name for ever…9 **So Manasseh made Judah and the inhabitants of Jerusalem to err, and to do worse than the heathen, whom the LORD had destroyed before the children of Israel.** 10 And the LORD spake to Manasseh, and to his people: but they would not hearken."

From the above scriptures, we can see that King Manasseh practiced **witchcraft, enchantments**, and he **used wizards** and **familiar spirits** to carry out his ungodly activities. We can also see that King Manasseh defiled the house of the Lord by bringing idolatry into it and he made the children of Israel to sin with his promotion of idolatry. By following the ways of King Jeroboam and by doing the things that he knew God hated, King Manasseh brought the wrath of God upon himself and his house.

King Ahab and Jezebel Practiced Witchcraft

King Ahab and His wife Jezebel also practiced witchcraft in northern Israel. We can see this from God's judgment against the house of Ahab and against his wife, Jezebel. It also shows in the statement that Captain Jehu made to King Joram (Ahab and Jezebel's son) when he came to execute God's judgment against him in **2 Kings 9:22-24**:

"And it came to pass, when Joram saw Jehu, that he said, Is it peace, Jehu? And he answered, **What peace, so long as the whoredoms of thy mother Jezebel and her witchcrafts are so many?** 23 And Joram turned his hands, and fled, and said to Ahaziah, There is treachery, O Ahaziah. 24 And Jehu drew a bow with his full strength, and smote Jehoram between his arms, and the arrow went out at his heart, and he sunk down in his chariot."

Chapter 3
Tools of the Witchcraft Spirit

Use of Soothsaying or Predictions

From the time that God brought the children of Israel out of Egypt, He also began the work of eliminating idolatry from them as we see in **Micah 5:12-13**. It was clear to the children of Israel that God was determined to stamp out the practice of witchcraft in all of Israel:

> **"And I will cut off witchcrafts out of thine hand; and thou shalt have no more <u>soothsayers</u>:** 13 Thy graven images also will I cut off, and thy standing images out of the midst of thee; and thou shalt no more worship the work of thine hands."

There is a new addition to the tools of witchcraft that is highlighted in the above scripture — soothsaying. What is soothsaying? **Soothsaying is the art of 'foretelling' events or 'making predictions' by the help of familiar spirits.** This is why some people consult <u>psychics</u> or fortune tellers for some reading. These agents of the devil openly make use of familiar spirits in their soothsaying and in their other demonic activities. One of the most notable soothsayers is the man called **Nostradamus**. His profession besides his practice of medicine was giving 'psychic readings', astrology and other occultic activities. His predictions were considered to be demonically inspired because he was not being led by the Holy Spirit. During his lifetime, he feared being burnt at the stakes because people considered his occultic activities to be against biblical teachings.

When you look at some of Nostradamus predictions, you might think he was accurate in what he predicted but what you must remember is that the devil has always had plans against humanity. **All the devil did was to announce his plans ahead of time through Nostradamus who yielded**

himself to him. Therefore, you cannot say that just because the destructive wars and whatever else it was that Nostradamus predicted came to pass means that he was right. The devil just used him to announce what he was going to do. There are still people like Nostradamus today that practice fortune telling, divinations and palm reading with the use of their 'physic power' but all these are tools of the witchcraft spirit.

In this country, there is a large pool of psychics that charge people money for giving them a reading or making predictions for them. As Christians, we are not to deal with them because they are not from the Spirit of God; they are using the aids of familiar spirits. **The only true and accurate predictions are the ones that come from the Holy Spirit.** Any prediction outside of the Holy Spirit cannot be received by a true Christian because they represent covenants with familiar spirits.

Activities of Familiar Spirits
Familiar spirits are evil spirits that can assume the physical features of dead people and then pretend to be the people as they deal with members of the people's families. They are the devil's messengers and they are a part of the devil's tools of deception. I wrote about them in one of my books titled, *How to Discern and Expel Evil Spirits; Chapter 3* and below is an excerpt that might be of help to you:

> *"For example, there is a class of evil spirits that are called 'familiar spirits'. They are spirits that are sent by the devil to do his bidding. Always remember that the **pre-Adamic beings** (the former inhabitants of the earth that are now devils) willingly yielded themselves to the devil and as result, he is now their lord. He tells them what to do. They have become totally enslaved by him and they have totally taken on the nature of the devil. He sends them into families to monitor the members and to carry out his evil intentions against the family. This is why the root word is '**familidris**' or*

'familia' which in Latin means family. They are sent into a particular family to operate in that family alone.

When familiar spirits come into a family they monitor the habits, they monitor the dislikes and they monitor the lives of the members of the family. Why? Because they have to effectively 'misrepresent' you to somebody in a vision or a dream. This is why you sometimes hear someone saying that somebody that had died in his or her family came back to him or her in a vision or in a dream and they're talking to the dead person. Some familiar spirits even give such people counsel in visions and dreams.

When you see your dead relative in a vision or dream, know that you are dealing with a familiar spirit that monitored the habits of that dead relative and knows how that relative operated in their lifetime and now wants to portray that relative to you. Why? Because they lost their home (the body of that dead relative) and so the spirits are now looking for the next person who will welcome them into their body..."

Familiar spirits will tell you whatever it is that you want to hear just so you can be a loyal patron or customer who keeps coming back as they distract you away from God.

The End Does Not Justify the Means

Those who make predictions without the Holy Spirit are called false prophets even if their predictions come to pass. As we already saw, the devil uses them to announce his plans hence they come to pass. The Lord asked me, **"Does the end justify the means?"** I said, "No" and He said that I should always identify the spirit working through a person. Biblically speaking, it means that a prediction that is not by the Holy Spirit is not acceptable to God and it is not to be accepted by us even if the outcome is good. This confirms what the Lord said in **Matthew 7:15-20** that a corrupt tree cannot bring forth good fruit:

"**Beware of false prophets**, which come to you in sheep's clothing, but inwardly they are ravening wolves. *16* **Ye shall know them by their fruits. Do men gather grapes of thorns, or figs of thistles?** *17* Even so every good tree bringeth forth good fruit; but a corrupt tree bringeth forth evil fruit. *18* **A good tree cannot bring forth evil fruit, neither can a corrupt tree bring forth good fruit.** *19* Every tree that bringeth not forth good fruit is hewn down, and cast into the fire. *20* **Wherefore by their fruits ye shall know them.**"

This principle also applies to every spiritual encounter that you experience. For example, when you go to a church, look to see by what spirit the church is operating so that you do not get deceived. Even speaking in tongues has to be by the Holy Spirit; you also have to confirm the speaking in tongues to be of the Holy Spirit. **I say this because not all 'Christian churches' belong to the Lord. When I go to Africa, I sometimes encountered some witchdoctors and those who 'perform cure' with demonic powers. Some of them have told me that they come to churches in the United States to 'perform cure'.** I will discuss this in a later chapter titled, **Characteristics of the Different Types of Witchcrafts.**

I often wondered about the type of churches that invite them. **To me, it was obvious that any church that would invite a witchdoctor or one who 'performs cure' with demonic powers is not a discerning church.** They obviously equate 'performing cure' with healing by the Holy Spirit without identifying the source of the power. Therefore, you have to learn to judge a spirit by the Word of God to see if it is of God. In other words, you must judge the root of the spirit to see if it is the Spirit of the Lord or if it is of a satanic power.

Also, you have some people who claim to be 'white' or 'good' witches but the truth of the matter is that there is no such thing. Some of them are given access into churches by leaders and we know that they do not function with the power of the Holy Spirit. Never forget what the Lord said about the devil's kingdom. The devil recycles events and afflictions because he will not cast out his own demons. Doing so will make his kingdom to become divided and according to the Lord, a divided kingdom cannot stand — **Matthew 12:25-26:**

"And Jesus knew their thoughts, and said unto them, **Every kingdom divided against itself is brought to desolation**; and every city or house divided against itself shall not stand: 26 **And if Satan cast out Satan, he is divided against himself; how shall then his kingdom stand?**... He that is not with me is against me; and he that gathereth not with me scattereth abroad."

The Lord Jesus then went on to let us know that **he that is not with Him is against Him and he that does not build with Him scatters.** As a result, when you go into a church, it matters what spirit the preacher is operating by lest you become ensnared by the devil. When you perceive that the spirit by which he or she is operating is not of the Lord, run. The devil uses false miracles, and lying signs and wonders to deceive people to believe in his evil and demonically inspired activities. When the **anti-Christ** shows up, you will see his **false prophet** calling fire down from heaven and will make the image of the anti-Christ (the beast) to speak — **Revelation 13:11-15:**

"**And I beheld another beast coming up out of the earth; and he had two horns like a lamb, and he spake as a dragon.** 12 And he exerciseth all the power of the first beast before him, and causeth the earth and them which dwell therein to worship the first beast, whose deadly wound was healed. 13 **And he doeth great wonders,** so that **he maketh fire come down from heaven** on the earth in the sight of men, 14 **And deceiveth them that dwell on the earth by**

the means of those miracles which he had power to do in the sight of the beast; saying to them that dwell on the earth, that they should make an image to the beast, which had the wound by a sword, and did live. 15 And he had power to give life unto the image of the beast, that the image of the beast should both speak, and cause that as many as would not worship the image of the beast should be killed."

Do not be deceived just because you saw a miracle because the source of the miracle matters. As evidence of the truth of the above scripture and as we examine the different types of witchcraft practices, you will see that all their fruit is evil. **The reason is because satan is the root of all forms of witchcraft.**

How People Get Involved in Witchcraft through Idolatry

Man was created by God to worship Him and when man fell away from God through sin, he did not lose his desire or abilities to worship. Therefore, in the absence of God, the devil will help man to find something to worship. The Lord once said to me, "Man is a very intelligent being you know." And he proceeded to ask me the following question: **"What do you think would make a man to bow down to a rock or to a tree? Something has to have happened to the tree because man is not stupid."** He gave me the following example: If a man is walking by a tree and the tree suddenly lights up and begins to shine or to wink at him, the man would want to investigate the occurrence but to the devil, he just got the man's attention. The next thing you know, the man will begin to consult the tree for guidance and before long, the man falls into idolatry.

As a result, where there is already an evil root of idolatry or ungodly religious rituals, the devil likes to put on a show of demonic display for the people through the use of objects. **For example, the devil will use his demons to make statues** to bleed for you if you live in a place where such occurrence is reverenced or if you belong to the church denomination that uses such occurrences to attract mass pilgrims. The demons would make sure that when the people visit a statue, it would begin to bleed because they are fascinated by their display. In reality, all the demons did was to go into the statue and put on a display for the visitors! **As they put on these displays, they are in essence evangelizing people to believe in the idolatry as they make drops of blood flow from the statues to the people's amazement**.

These unsuspecting people will begin to venerate the statues without realizing that they have just been recruited into the devil's web of idolatry and witchcraft. Today, many people all over the world go to certain locations across the globe to see these things and the devil is more than glad to oblige them. **He is pleased that he got their attention because he knows that while they are getting involved in this form of idolatry, they are becoming abominable in the sight of God**; the devil is no dummy. The Bible tells us in **Isaiah 41:23-24** that those who practice idolatry are abominable to God:

"Shew the things that are to come hereafter, that we may know that ye are gods *(idols)*: yea, do good, or do evil, that we may be dismayed, and behold it together. 24 **Behold, ye** *(idols)* **are of nothing, and your work of nought**: an abomination is he that chooseth you."

The Devil's Attempt to Recruit Me into Idolatry

Personally, I have seen pictures on magazine covers that winked at me or that smiled at me at the grocery stores or at people's homes and I always rebuke them. The first incident happened in my apartment and below is my narration of it:

When I was newly 'born again', I was at a book store and I saw a very good artistic painting of the 'face of the Lord Jesus' with His head tilted back and a very broad smile on His face. I thought that it was a very good picture of how the Lord might look when He is in a very relaxed and playful mode so I decided to buy it. I took it to my apartment and as I was about to hang it on the wall in my living room, I heard the Lord say, "That is not Me." I guess I was too young in the Lord to take what He said to me to heart. As you can guess, I had not learned the importance of obedience to the Word of God yet so, I went ahead and hung it on the wall.

*One day, I came into my apartment and I was walking by the picture on the way to my bedroom and **it winked at me**! I was shocked that a picture can wink at a person so I decided that it must have been my imagination and went on. After a few days, I was walking by the picture and **it again winked at me but this time, it held the wink for a while before releasing it** and I could not believe what had just happened. As I stood there wondering about it, the Lord said to me, "I told you that, that was not me; keep your eyes on me and not a picture." I immediately removed the picture from the wall and tore it up.*

Afterwards, the Lord began to show me that because putting up the picture was a form of idolatry, an evil spirit went into it to put on a show for me in the devil's attempt to get me to worship or reverence the picture! Therefore, be aware that evil spirits can easily enter into objects to get people's attention and to recruit them into idolatry. This is why the Lord told us not to have any graven images in our homes.

In the next chapters, we are going to examine the different types of witchcrafts beginning with satanic covens and the West African type of witchcraft.

Chapter 4
Satanic Covens and the Satanic Church

There are several types of witchcrafts and although **they are all rooted in wickedness,** their operations are different. **The witchcraft spirit is a spirit that knows how to adapt itself to different cultures, countries and people groups. As a result, the operation of the witchcraft spirit varies in different societies and each has its own unique flavor of activities but their end is all the same — destruction!** A lot of Christians have had assignments sent against them from satanic covens or by satanists. Therefore, we need to understand who they are and what they do.

In a satanic coven, a group of people agree to form an assembly in order to practice witchcraft and to worship satan. Their activities are based on the worship of satan and their rituals or rites involve various evil things. The most popular are the **use of blood, sexual abuse, saying of the 'black mass', hatred of Christians, casting of spells, channeling of thoughts, evil meditation** and **use of magic.**

Use of Blood in Human and Animal Sacrifices
The use of human and animal blood in satanic rituals is a common knowledge in most societies around the world. **The lower level rituals only involve the use of animal blood but just like a witchdoctor, those who are higher up in satanic organizations require the use of human blood in their more serious rituals.** They drink the blood as part of their rituals, eat some of the body parts and use the remaining parts for other evil rites. It is the most secretive part of their rituals and members of satanic coven will not publicly admit to its existence.

According to a report that I read not long ago, thousands of people are sacrificed annually by satanists in the U.S. alone. **The report stated that this is one of the reasons why**

some missing people are never found. Since satanists give themselves wholly over to the devil, he can use them to carry out these evil activities without moral condemnation by their conscience. They are deceived by him and cannot see that they are 'axis of evil' in a world already plagued by wickedness. There are accounts of people that have escaped their gruesome encounters in satanic rituals and some of them tell of how they watched as people were being sacrificed in the worship of satan.

Use of Sexual Abuse

The same report had accounts of young girls that were kidnapped, raped or forced into satanic marriages. Sexual child abuse that sometimes involve the parents of the children is common in satanic rituals. According to the report, some of the girls' parents who themselves were active satanists, were present when the girls were forced into satanic marriages in public rape ceremonies as a form of the worship of satan. There are also accounts of satanic parents who conceive a baby girl and raise her up just to be married to satan in a satanic child abuse or public rape.

Saying of 'Black Mass'

The 'black mass' is believed to be a ritual characterized by the **inversion** (reversal or order) of the traditional **Latin Mass** celebrated by the Roman Catholic Church. It is celebrated during the 'witches' sabbath' or 'gathering'. The church of satan has a publication on the rituals or steps for conducting 'black mass'. Both the church of satan and satanic covens are institutions that worship satan and delight in devilish activities.

They like to do the opposite of what the Word of God says and they enjoy publicly defying the ways of God that are outlined in the Bible. For example, they use a cross that is turned upside down just as they like to turn the things of God upside down. Their 'black mass' is purely from the pit of hell.

Strong Hatred of the God of the Bible and Christians

As a Christian or a minister, you are going to teach, say or preach things that challenge both the satanic church and satanic covens. Therefore, be aware of any satanic covens or small satanic groups in your neighborhood. Satanists like to infiltrate churches so that they can try to harm the ministers and the members. **As 'born again' Christians, we are way above them and we have God's own power and authority over them.** The blood of Jesus destroys all and any assignment that they might send against you so never be afraid of them. This is why we need to invoke the blood of Jesus during our services because the blood of Jesus destroys their activities.

When you suspect a person in your church of being involved in satanism, ask the person if he or she believes and confesses that the Lord Jesus Christ is Lord of all. Also, watch the person during prayers sessions to make sure that he or she does not chant satanic verses in your Christian gatherings. The reason for this is because they like to go into churches to cast spells or carryout wicked assignments against the pastor and against the congregation. Again, always remember the power of the blood of Jesus and the fact that if they try to harm you, they will fall into the pit that they tried to dig for you. One word from a Spirit-filled Christian and they can drop dead!

Use of Black Magic and White Magic

When I talk about magic here, I am not talking about the magician who uses illusion to entertain people but about wicked men and women who use demonic powers to make certain evil things happen. **Magic is defined as the practice of controlling or forecasting natural events, effects, or forces by invoking the supernatural.** The practice involves using charms, spells, or rituals to attempt to produce supernatural effects or control events in nature. **'Black magic' is the use of supernatural powers or magic for evil and selfish purposes.** The satanists use it to produce evil effects on their victims. The so-called **'white magic'** involves the practice of incantation for 'good purposes' such as providing a cure or as a counter to the negative effects of 'black magic'.

Do not be deceived by the claim of 'white magic' because both white and black magic come from the same source — the devil! We again have to remember the words of the Lord that a house divided against itself cannot stand. Therefore, there are people that the devil deceives into believing that they are doing good but they are like the witchdoctors who believe that thay are using their evil powers to do 'good'.

Casting of Spells

Satanists use spell casting in their satanic activities. They use evocation to bind someone with a spell with words spoken in a formula. Spells are believed by those who practice them to be a form of communication between human beings and spirits as they seek the intervention of the spirits for good or evil. By casting the spell, they are asking the spirits to influence the thoughts and deeds of others. They themselves have totally given their mind over to the devil and he makes them believe that they can use their minds to influence others.

As a result, they try to send people evil thoughts and spells in order to control their actions. We cannot be programmed by satanists as we walk with the **mind of Christ** and as we plead the blood of Jesus over our minds and over our thoughts. In Christ Jesus, we who are 'born again' have total victory over the devil and his spell casting agents. This is why we are told the following in **Ephesians 6:10-18**:

> "**Finally, my brethren, be <u>strong in the Lord</u>, and in the <u>power of his might</u>.** *11* Put on the whole armour of God, that ye may be able to stand against the wiles of the devil. *12* For we wrestle not against flesh and blood *(human beings)*, but against **principalities, against powers,** against the **rulers of the darkness** of this world *(occultic spirits)*, against **spiritual wickedness** in

high places. *13* Wherefore take unto you the whole armour of God, that ye may be able to withstand in the evil day, and having done all, to stand.

14 Stand therefore, having **your loins girt about with truth**, and having on the **breastplate of righteousness**; *15* And **your feet shod with the preparation of the gospel of peace**; *16* Above all, **taking the shield of faith**, wherewith ye shall be able to quench all the fiery darts of the wicked. *17* And take the helmet of salvation, and the sword of the Spirit, which is the word of God: *18* Praying always with all prayer and supplication in the Spirit..."

Our shield of faith is the Word of God (both Living and Written) that prevails over any evil force. **Therefore, we are not afraid of satanic spells and charms because the Word of God says that in Christ, we forever have the victory over them all.**

Channeling of Thoughts

This is a process in which a person becomes a medium through which evil spirits can give messages or thoughts for themselves or for other people. In other words, it is an attempts to give messages received through thoughts from an evil spirit. Those who channel their thoughts claim to speak for spirit beings operating through them but the unfortunate thing is that they are dealing with evil spirits that will eventually destroy them.

Meanwhile, they are being deceived by the devil because before they can operate as mediums to channel their thoughts, they must give complete control of their mind to him through his evil spirits. This why they have to empty their mind of any conscious thought before the evil spirit can speak through them. By so doing, they become one with the devil through his evil spirits.

Unfortunately, you now hear a lot of people talking freely about 'channeling' because it has been made popular by Hollywood in movies and TV programs. Also, it is now a common expression for those in the media to declare that they are 'channeling' their thoughts as they speak. As a result, a lot of people now think that is ok to 'channel' your thoughts but we who are Christians must always remember that it is a demonic practice and stay away from it.

Engage in Evil Meditation

Just like those who channel their thoughts, evil meditation also requires that those who practice it empty their mind of all thoughts. By doing this, they give complete control of their mind and body to evil spirits to occupy. It is a form of possession by evil spirits. Because I grew up in Africa, to me, most satanic covens are not sophisticated forms of witchcraft. Having said that, I immediately want to stress **that no form of witchcraft is a light thing;** even the seemingly elementary ones. The reason is because they involve active covenants with the devil and they involve evil sacrifices.

Sometimes during street evangelism, I run into witches in satanic covens and to their shock, I usually tell them that they do not know what satanic power is. I also ask them if they think that they have power just because they sacrifice cats and other animals. **I then proceed to tell them that even if they sacrifice a human being, they will still have a <u>mild form of witchcraft power</u> compared to the more powerful types in Africa and elsewhere.** While they are still in shock, I tell them that a witch that has to rely on a book and follow written procedures to exercise power is not a very powerful witch. Normally, they do not have anything to say to me after that but I tell them to seek the REAL POWER from JESUS!

As 'born again' Christians, we are not to be afraid of any form of witchcraft or any <u>witch</u> or <u>wizard</u> that rises up against us because the Lord Jesus has given us the authority

to tread upon them all (serpents and scorpions — evil spirits**) and to walk over all their power.** He also said that nothing shall by any means hurt us — **Luke 10:19:**

> "Behold, **I give unto you power to tread on serpents and scorpions, and over all the power of the enemy**: and **nothing shall by any means hurt you**."

Actually, witches and wizards fear true Christians because of the name and the blood of Jesus. They fear the Word of God.

One of My Encounters with Satanists

We were on street evangelism in Atlanta and my group and I were about to cross the street when the light turned red and I got separated from them because I was not able to cross over to the other side before the light changed. As a result, I was standing alone waiting for the light to change while the group waited for me on the other side of the street. As I stood there, I turned around just in time to see that there were a bunch of satanists that suddenly surrounded me. My first reaction was, oh no, these are male witches (wizards) because except for one of them, they all had on the satanic cloak and everything else. As soon as I realized who they were, I heard the voice of the Lord saying, "Do not be afraid."

My group saw that I was the only person in the mist of all these male witches so our evangelism leader decided that they were going to cross the street back to me in order to assist me, but he later told me that the Lord told him that I was Ok. Also, the Lord told him that they were not to cross the street back to me and that they should leave me alone. Therefore, they stood and watched me with the group of satanists on the other side of the street. I have never been one to back away from fights or confrontations so, I said to them, "Are you witches and wizards?" They said, "Yes," so I asked them, "You all are worshiping satan?" They said, "Yes." My reply was, "Is it not ridicules for you to worship satan?"

They wanted to know why I thought it was ridiculous and I asked them, "Have you ever seen a person on a leash and being walked by their dog; wouldn't that person look ridicules to you?" They agreed that it would be ridiculous so I said, "That is how you all look to me." **I began to explain to them that that God made them all in His image and not only that, He gave them dominion over everything that is upon the face of the earth; including the devil!** *I said to them that, "The Lord meant for you all to put the devil on a leash like a dog and command him to do your bidding and for you to control him like a dog but instead of you all putting the devil on a leash like a dog, you allow the devil to put you all on his leash and walk you about like a dog."* **I told them that they are supposed to be the devil's boss but instead, they are running around doing the devil's biddings and advertising for him! I told them that they are worshiping the very entity that they are supposed to tread upon and make jump at their commands.** *I informed them that they were lost and that they needed to get hold of the Lord so that they can find out who they are in Christ —* **Priests and Kings!** *By the time I was done, three of them received the Lord immediately. One of them was who being initiated said, "I am no longer with them" and I said that he made the right decision and that he needed to stay away from the other satanists.* **The leader of the satanic group became angry and told me that he could have done some serious harm to me but that he did not have his book.**

I told him that I would wait for him right where I was standing so that he can go and get the book because I wanted him to see the power of my Lord Jesus Christ. He then informed me that he was going to kill me that night. I said, "Whatever you do against me tonight, you are going to have an encounter with my Lord Jesus Christ." After this, I prayed over the ones (former satanists) that received the Lord and the one 'former initiate' that also got saved. In my prayer, I asked the Lord to be a hedge of protection around them so that the devil is not able to afflict them for deserting him and I told their former leader that if he should chant or do any incantations again them, the fire of the Lord will burn him and it will continue to burn him until he stops coming against them.

That day, I discovered that even when you find yourself in the mist of witches and wizards, you should stand your ground in faith with the Lord because He will keep you safe. I also saw His power to snatch souls from the devil and confound the enemy. Know therefore that He will make sure that witches cannot harm you because He said in **Luke 10:19** that, **"Nothing shall by any means hurt you."** This decree covers all Christians and it is forever.

Chapter 5
The West African Type of Witchcraft

The Power of the 'Born Again' Christian

When it comes to the West African type of witchcraft, I do not want you to be afraid of the information concerning it because **as a 'born again' Christian, you are kept by the Holy Spirit and the devil cannot harm you and he cannot give you that which you have said NO to.** Just remember to bless your food and speak peace to everywhere you go. Say NO to all forms of evil at all times. Also remember the Lord's power to rebuke anyone that tries to put witchcraft in your food.

Although I zeroed in on the West African type of witchcraft in this chapter, know that it is a model for all the other types of witchcrafts activities that are more lethal that have been imported from West Africa to other parts of Africa and the rest of the world. For obvious reasons that you will see later, it is the most wicked type of witchcraft and it hates anything good or progressive.

The West African Definition of a Witch

By <u>West African definition</u>, **a witch or a wizard is someone who belongs to a supernatural organization that conducts nightly meetings in the spirit realm and who possesses the <u>supernatural ability to eject their human soul into a bird or some other animal in order to fly</u> to attend these evil nightly meetings.** You can immediately see that this is different from people who are in satanic covens that practice evil sacrifices and spells using written formulas or incantations.

The West African type of witchcraft is centered on what they call their **'Queen of the Night'** who conducts nightly meetings in the spirit realm that all the witches and wizards must fly to attend. **Some of these meetings are held over the Atlantic Ocean, other bodies of water, towns, cities, states and nations around the globe.** Attending these meetings is the highest level of witchcraft activity and the most dangerous.

In West Africa, you are not a witch if you cannot fly. The reason for this is because witchcraft does not only happen in the physical realm alone; it happens also on a demonic level in the spiritual realm. **Therefore, a true witch has to be able to change or eject his or her human soul into a bird in order to go to the nightly gathering.**

Witches Are Blind and Do Not Recognize Love

When the witches transform themselves, they become totally blind, enjoy only evil and they have a serious hatred for all those who are not their fellow witches. They hate even their own children; especially the child who goes out of his or her way to help them financially or who happens to be doing well and prospering. They will tell you that while at their nightly gatherings, they lose consciousness of what goes on in the physical realm. As a result, they can initiate an assignment against their own children without knowing it! They only recognize their children that are fellow witches and wizards.

Besides being blind while they are at their evil nightly meetings, their preoccupation and loyalty is to their evil group. They do not recognize anything that is good, friends, love or kindness. I remember when I was growing up in Africa and how one day, a woman was screaming as she was confessing her witchcraft activities in order to avoid physical death. Although I was young, I can still recall some elderly people talking about the number of babies that had died at the time. In other words, too many babies were dying and according to the woman confessing her evil activities, she had been responsible for all the deaths!

She confessed that the reason her butt was large and bouncing was because she was using the heads of the dead babies to string the beads that she wore around her waist in the spirit realm as the queen of her own region. Every time we saw the lady afterwards, my dad's mother would make us avoid her by walking on the other side of the road. I heard later that the reason she confessed her evil deeds was because the parents of one of the dead babies had consulted a very powerful witchdoctor from another part of the state with higher ranking than hers and he made a decree that the person responsible for the death of the child would die within certain days if the person did not confess. She confessed and lived.

How People Become Witches or Wizards

A true witchcraft spirit is <u>not for sale</u> and <u>cannot be bought</u>. Any West African witch or wizard will tell you that you cannot pay money to become a witch because paying nullifies the power of the witchcraft spirit. **It is not for sale but <u>it is given to a person</u>. The problem is that they do not tell their intended recruit about their desire to turn him or her into a witch to fly with them at night!** The common way that they pass it on or give it to a person is through food!

What this means is that the West African type of witchcraft is usually passed from one person to another through food served to their victim. The devil regards a person's acceptance of the food as his or her <u>willingness</u> to receive his witchcraft spirit because the unsuspecting person 'ignorantly and willingly received the food.' **In this regard, the witchcraft spirit can only be a gift; an evil gift that does not leave the receiver a choice to reject it because the devil regards eating the food as the person's consent.** It violates the desire of its victims. This is why when people go to visit other people in Nigeria, they do not eat food from anyone that they do not trust not to be witch. Unless they paid for the food, most people will not eat outside of their home. **As children, we were warned never to accept food from anyone no matter how hungry we were so that someone does not put witchcraft in our food.**

As a result, I never ate a cooked meal outside of the home unless I paid for it. Even today, many people are very apprehensive about eating food from people that they do not know. **This is because the general belief is that if**

you do not want to fly, you better be careful of what you eat and where you eat. This is hard core witchcraft and an example of the devil's wickedness.

The Witches' Call to Flight at Night

A true witch flies and wants to take others with him or her in the night flights. In other words, witches want to take others on their flight the same way you invite a friend to go somewhere with you. Therefore, they ensnare their unsuspecting victims through food in order **to take them to their nightly meetings. They do this because once a person becomes a witch or a wizard by eating the food, the person cannot refuse to go on the nightly flights.** The first night after the person ate the witchcraft and goes to bed, he or she will begin to hear the **'witches' call'** and his or her <u>soul must respond by ejecting out of the body into a bird</u> to go on the flights. God called this part of witchcraft the hunting of human souls to make them fly in **Ezekiel 13:20:**

> "Wherefore thus saith the Lord GOD; **Behold, I am against <u>your pillows</u>, <u>wherewith ye there hunt the souls to make them fly,</u>** and I will tear them from your arms, **and will let the souls go, <u>even the souls that ye hunt to make them fly</u>**."

Once a person has been turned into a witch, the person's soul begins to fly at night without any ability to stop it unless he or she turns to Christ. **Only the Lord Jesus can set a person free from the witchcraft spirit.** Growing up, there were regular accounts of people that had eaten food containing witchcraft and began to enter into birds to fly at night and they cried out the next morning because it was not their desire to become witches. As a result, it was not uncommon to see two people fighting in the early hours of the morning because one of them had put witchcraft in the other's meal and took them on a flight that the victim did not want to embark on.

They fight because the victim now has no choice when he or she is called but to fly. **It gets worse because if when**

at the evil nightly meetings in the realm of the spirit; he or she is offered human flesh and eats, he or she also has to reciprocate by providing a member of his or her family (usually the good person in the family) to be eaten by the group in return. I will talk about this in the subtitle that talks about the **'Lure or Crave for Human Flesh'.**

Also, once a person has been turned into a witch or a wizard, not only will the person have to respond to the 'witches call' every night, <u>he or she gets to pass it on to his or her next generation through the bloodline.</u> **Even when the person dies, 'the call' will still be issued to his or her children to come join the nightly flight as a form of inheritance.** This is because the hierarchical position in witchcraft is bequeathed but not all those who carry the spirit in their bloodline fly. Therefore, although you are not a witch or have never had any dealing with witchcraft practice, it does not stop them from calling your name in recognition of the covenant that your ancestor had with them.

For example, have you ever been alone and heard someone call your name? Do you sometimes hear your name being called and you ask the person around you if he or she called you and they say no? As 'born again' Christians, when this is happening, it is an indication that there was an active witchcraft practice in our bloodline because the positions and the titles in the hierarchy of the witches and wizards are passed on to the children. They must renounce this covenant and whatever position that was passed on to them in the hierarchy of witchcraft by the previous generations. There is another part of this 'witches call' that I will discuss later because it has to do with evil assignments.

The Toll of the Nightly Flights on the Human Body

There are some witches that do not want to weary their souls in long distance flights and as a result, pick a victim (usually a person <u>who is not</u> a witch or a wizard) and ride on the victim's soul for the nightly flights. Sometimes, the flights take them over the Atlantic Ocean or to other nations! This is why when you are being attacked by the West African type of witchcraft, you can wake up in the morning feeling as though you ran a marathon even after you had 8-9 hours of uninterrupted sleep. Your soul is where you record your memories and your feelings. It is the part of your brain that tells your body to be tired.

Unbelievers who have witchcraft in their bloodline are sometimes vulnerable to witches or wizards in their families who 'borrow' their souls for the nightly flights. Therefore, when you get unreasonably tired in the morning even after sleeping more than 8 hours at night, you may be under the attack of a witch or a wizard who is wearing down your soul by flying with it at night. They usually pick their family members to do this with but once you give your life to the Lord Jesus (become born again) and renounce the witchcraft in your bloodline, they will no longer be able to penetrate your soul.

The Lure or Crave for Human Flesh

One of the wicked aspects of the West African witches and wizards is that they crave human flesh. In other words, they have to have human meat as a meal every night and this makes it a more serious type of witchcraft. **The result is that they kill people on a nightly basis since human flesh is a nightly staple at their meetings in the realm of the spirit.** They are able to plot evil, to send sicknesses and disease and death against those that they perceive to be their enemies. **The problem is that anyone who is not their fellow witch or wizard is an enemy to them; even their own children!**

As a result, when a newly recruited witch or wizard eventually losses his or her strength to resist eating human flesh, they become indebted to provide a soul for them to eat at the nightly meetings. In other words, once the person partakes of eating human flesh, the person must also deliver a person (usually a prized family member) to the group for them to eat. When a person has been delivered up to the witches' group by their family member as a potential victim, the witches still cannot kill the person unless the person responds to their 'call'. **Meaning that before they are able to kill someone, they have to get the person to respond to their 'call'.** Remember what I said about hearing your name being called when no one is around or when those around you are not calling you? This is a 'call' to make a person give his or her consent to an evil assignment.

The person supposedly gives his or her consent to their intentions by responding to his or her name being called without checking to see if someone around them was truly calling them. It is one of the reasons why in West Africa, when you hear your name being called and no one is around, you do not respond. If you had responded and then discovered that no one around you had called you, you immediately cancel your response to the 'call'. It is the devil's way of counterfeiting the Lord's calls to Christians.

We that are 'born again' do not have to be afraid of the devil's 'evil call' because we are the ones that have the power to decree what we want to happen in our lives. You can always erase every evil call; praise the Lord. **Also as Christians, ask the Lord to hide your name in the thunder of His voice so that when anyone calls your name for evil the thunder of His voice will answer them on your behalf.**

The Witchdoctors as 'Good Witches and Wizards'

Most witchdoctors do not disclaim the fact that they are witches or wizards but they regard themselves as the 'good witches' or the 'good wizards.' The reason is because they claim to use their powers to cure people but they will kill someone if their services are requested. They can also attend the nightly meetings on behalf of their clients for certain requested services; even to help kill, maim or make a person sick.

While I was growing up in Africa, most of the witchdoctors that we came across always maintain their claim of being the 'good witches or wizards' because they had never eaten any human flesh. They had pride in their ability to resist the witches' crave to eat human flesh at their nightly gatherings. As a result, they saw themselves as using their power to do good and not evil but we know that when it comes to the devil, there is nothing good in any association with him.

I once spoke to someone who told me that he was a witch but that he was the 'good witch' because although he attends the nightly meetings, he has never eaten any human flesh. Therefore, he was not under any obligation to deliver up anyone from his family to them. According to him, the other witches listen to him when an assignment is sent against someone and he can bargain with them for the life of the person. **He informed me that the desire to eat human flesh is almost irresistible while at the meeting but once a person tastes human flesh, the person cannot stop the craving for it.** Those who eat human flesh become very evil and destructive. He believed that he was using his witchcraft power for good but we know that in **Matthew 7:16-18**, Jesus said that a corrupt tree cannot bring forth good fruit:

> **"Ye shall know them by their fruits.** Do men gather grapes of thorns, or figs of thistles? 17 **Even so every good tree bringeth forth good fruit; but a corrupt tree bringeth forth evil fruit.** 18 **A good tree cannot bring forth evil fruit, neither can a corrupt tree bring forth good fruit."**

The tree of witchcraft is a corrupt tree and no good thing can ever come of it. Therefore, do not let anyone deceive you by saying that he or she is a 'good witch' because there is no such thing. I know that they are now marketing movies and TV shows about the 'good witch' to the public; movies such as Harry Potter, The Witches of Eastwick, The Covenant, Dark Shadows, etc., but do not fall for them. Their root is demonic.

Keeping Cats and Dogs as Pets

One of the things that you will notice when you visit some countries in Africa is that most people (especially young people) do not keep cats and dogs as pets. One of the reasons for this is that witches and wizards have a notorious reputation of ejecting their souls into cats, birds, and dogs in their efforts to harm people. If they cannot come into your house during the night, then they come in through your cat or dog. As a result, most people do not keep pets so that the witches and wizards do not come into their homes through them. As a young person, if you want people to avoid you like a plague when you visit parts of West Africa, then keep a cat as a pet. I was really shocked when I came to this country and I saw young people not only keeping cats and dogs as pets, but they carry their dogs around in their cars! It is something I never saw all the while I was growing up in Africa.

I always thought that it was superstitious to believe that witches' souls can enter into animals until I became 'born again' and God started using me in the ministry of deliverance. As I go into different people's homes, I discovered that the spirits of infirmities operate just like the witchcraft spirit through animals. **I believe that about 90% of those who have pets and are constantly battling one form of illness or another, get it through their cat or their dog!** On many occasions, I have had to rebuke the spirits in many people's pets as they try to spew sicknesses or diseases against me during my visit. I know that this is hard for Christian pet lovers but if you decide to keep a pet, you had better cover that pet with prayers on a regular basis because truly, evil spirits do get into animals to vex their owners. If they cannot get to you, they will target your pet because they need a foothold in your house.

Being Pressed by Witches on Your Bed

The West African witches and wizards will sometimes fly across the Atlantic Ocean to other countries to carry out assignments against their intended victims. This is why unsuspecting victims will sometimes see a 'black figure' or a shadowy figure in their bedrooms. **Some feel something or some entity pressing them down on their bed at night.** If the intended victim is not yet 'born again', they can try to kill him or her. **When the intended victim is a 'born again' Christian, he or she would sometimes wake up just in time to hear their human spirit rebuking or fighting against the witch or wizard.**

If the Christian is 'born again' but does not spend time in reading the Word of God, he or <u>she will feel the pressing of a witch or wizard but cannot respond</u> because the body is a lump of clay; **it is the human spirit that fights and its strength is the Word of God!** Personally, I have had to rebuke witches and wizards at night from my bedroom on many occasions until the Lord revealed this part of their activities through the bloodline to me. **Now, I plead the blood of Jesus over me before going to bed and they are unable to press me down on my bed anymore.** Sometimes, the Lord will let me know who the witch or wizard is that came against me by showing the person to me as he or she is flying away as a bird. It is usually amazing because I will see the bird flying away in the way that the person walks in real life!

On one occasion, I was going to speak death to the bird as it was going away but as I watched it, I could see that it was someone very close to me. I also realized that if I speak death to the bird and the person dies in real life, I will be the one to pay for the funeral because of how close the person was to me. In other words, this person was a very close relative.

The Request to Kill

Witches cannot just up and kill a person. There has to be a formal request made to kill the person and it must be signed off on by a member of the intended victim's family. According to several witches that have confessed their wicked deeds at their nightly gatherings, they usually receive a request to kill and eat a person from the person's family member who is their fellow witch. Once, the request is accepted, they will kill and eat the victim. **Soon after the person has been eaten by them spiritually, the person will then physically get sick and die or the person will get involved in a fatal accident.**

When I was growing up, it was not uncommon to hear that someone was confessing their guilt or regret for taking part in eating a person that had just died at their witches' nightly meeting. A lot of them claimed that they have been told to confess their part in killing or eating the person lest they too die like the person. **Some even claimed to have human flesh or bone lodged in their throat because they took part in eating the wrong victim or a victim that was truly a good person.** As a result, they must confess or they will die.

The West African witches and wizards are filled with envy and jealousy against anyone who is doing well in life. They are pleased when someone is sick or destitute because they hate:

- Joy or happiness
- Progress
- Prosperity
- Promotion
- Success
- Morality or Moral Uprightness

Because of their hatred for progress, prosperity and success, they are out to eliminate those around them that are prosperous. As a result, while at their evil nightly meetings, they will submit the names of their friends or family members who shared their future plans of prosperity with them. **The one who submitted the name will then request the help of the group to destroy the potential prosperity of the person or to kill the person.** In other words, they love to see people go through poverty and hardship and when they see anyone on the verge of breaking free from the cycle of poverty and hardship, they will immediately move to stop or kill the person.

These witches and wizards are rooted in the worship of satan via their evil 'Queen of the Night' and in return satan blinds them at their nightly meetings so that they are not able to appreciate anything good. **He makes them to desire only evil and it is only when they wake up in the morning that they realize the evil that they did in the night.** As a result, it was not uncommon as I stated before to see a mother crying in the morning because while she was at the evil nightly meeting, she delivered up her child for destruction and it is usually the good child or the bread winner who was providing for her needs.

Again, witches cannot just go after a person from another family without a 'request to kill' from a member of the family. Therefore, they will only receive an assignment against a person when it is presented by a member of the person's family; no outsider can present an assignment without the consent of someone from the potential victim's family approving it. **In other words, it takes a person from someone's family delivering the person up at the nightly meetings before the person can be killed!** So, before they can kill someone, there has to be a witch in the person's family that agrees to the assignment and it is this person that will essentially deliver the person up to be killed.

Once the assignment has been agreed upon, they will then go across the globe to carry it out. **Since they are not 'All-knowing', they do not know about your achievements or your impending success until you tell one of their agents or until they see you display your success like a new home or a new car.** Anyone who has a witchcraft spirit in their bloodline can be an agent (a peeper) of reporting to the devil all impending good things or prosperity that are shared with them. As a result, whatever good news anyone shares with them becomes an object to be attacked and destroyed. They essentially become spies for the devil without knowing it.

Chapter 6
Ways Witchcraft Spirit Oppress Its Victims

No Assignment against 'Born Again' Christians

Before I continue, I want to **reassure** all **'born again'**
Christians not to be afraid of the witchcraft spirit because the
good news over us is that we have the ability to destroy them
when we pray or make decrees using the Word of God. This is
why any witch or wizard will tell you that if anyone brings an
assignment against a 'born again' Christian at their meetings,
they usually turn it down. It is when you do not pray that you
leave room for them to harass or vex you. **They fear praying**
Christians. According to them, the fire around a 'born again'
person burns them and the blood of the Lord Jesus torments
them. As a result, they do not go near 'born again' Christians;
especially if they pray. The worst they can do is press you on
your bed when there is an open door (covenant) to them from
your bloodline but they cannot kill you.

They will also tell you that the only people that they are
afraid of in the whole world are 'born again' Christians.
Therefore, if you are a 'born again' Christian, do not be
afraid of them because the blood of Jesus is their nightmare
and it protects you. **Also, as a 'born again' Christian, when**
you plead the blood of Jesus and call the name of the Lord
Jesus on your food or bless the food in the name of Jesus,
no witchcraft can survive in the food. Whenever I visit an
African country, I shock people when I bless my food and eat
it without fear. I can do this because the Word of God over us
in **Mark 16:18** says:

> "They shall take up serpents; **and if they drink any**
> **deadly thing, it shall not hurt them;** they shall lay
> hands on the sick, and they shall recover."

And also in **Luke 10:19:**

> "**Behold, I give unto you power** to tread on serpents
> and scorpions, and **over all the power of the enemy**:
> **and nothing shall by any means hurt you.**"

Therefore, we do not walk in fear and we do not get intimidated by people who are or who claim to be witches. **The witches themselves know that the authority and the power in those who belong to Jesus Christ is greater than theirs. As a result, it is the only power that they fear.** I remember the Lord rebuking me once because I was in a bus sitting next to a witchdoctor in his full regalia and I folded my hands into my body in my attempt not to touch him and him not touch me. When I did this, he just spread himself wide on the seat to squeeze me in and **the Lord said to me, "Excuse me, between you and this man who has the most power?" I said, "I do" and He said, "So, act like it."** I immediately unfolded my hands and spread myself out. The witchdoctor began to fold himself in his attempt to get away from me. Everyone that is 'born again' has been given tremendous power by the Holy Spirit.

Witches and Wizards that Peep and Mutter

To **peep or peer is to look into something** but in this case, it means to look into people's lives and to make a report to the devil and his evil spirits. **These witches and wizards mutter or speak what they see to evil spirits.** They can pass on this aspect of their evil nature to their children and their children's children up to the 4th generation. This is why many people do not know that they are carriers of these types of spirits; especially if they are two or three generations away from the actual person that was a witch or a wizard in their bloodline. **The unfortunate thing is that as long as they are carriers of these spirits, the devil still sees them as his agents.**

The reason is because one of the things that witches and wizards do is **peep and mutter** and he does not exempt their children. Like the **"Peeping Toms"** who monitor or spy on people's privacy, these are monitoring spirits that spy on people's secret lives. If these spirits are in your bloodline, they will spy on or monitor your activities as well as the activities of those around you so that they can sabotage them. **They**

will mutter or whisper things into your ears in the nighttime because they are trying to train you to develop a negative thinking pattern. This practice is stated in **Isaiah 8:19** that we should stay away from people with familiar spirits and from witches and wizards that peep and mutter because they are spies for the devil:

> "And when they shall say unto you, **Seek unto them that have familiar spirits**, and unto **wizards that peep**, and **that mutter**: should not a people seek unto their God? for the living to the dead?"

There are people who just <u>mutter things to themselves</u> all day long as a form of mental affliction. **Many of their relatives do not recognize this activity of the witchcraft spirit when their loved one begins to speak to him or herself or to invisible things.** In other words, they are not able to discern that they are dealing with the witchcraft spirit but this type of affliction is very common. **It is one of the reasons why when you visit a psychiatric hospital, you see a lot of people speaking to themselves or to invisible things, while some smile at invisible objects all day long. There are those who spend the whole day repeating the things that the witchcraft spirit whispered or muttered into their ears while they were sleeping.**

A lot of the things that they speak are negative confessions because the evil spirits give them negative words intended to cancel all the good confessions that they were previously speaking over themselves and others. **The devil's strategy is to use their tongues to steal or erase their good confessions so that good things do not come to pass in their lives.** It is a destructive demonic assignment by the witchcraft spirit and <u>this group of people are usually the hardest to set free because they can use their tongue to erase words of deliverance spoken over them.</u>

Eavesdropping Spirits

Just like the **peeping tom spirits**, the 'eavesdropping' **spirits** also spy out people's activities. These spirits are also responsible for killing off any good prospects that are about to happen to those who are vulnerable to them because their job is to make sure that nothing good comes their way. **For example, a person can have a very promising or a good job interview and come away with an assurance from the interviewer that the job is going to be offered to them but the minute the person speaks about the prospect to someone who <u>carries an eavesdropping</u> or Peeping Tom spirit, the job offer fizzles away. The job offer fizzles away because the eavesdropping or spying spirit immediately reported the prospect of a good job offer to the devil and his agents and they killed it.**

A lot of people <u>speak their plans</u> to their friends or family members without knowing that the people's bloodline have 'open doors' to the witchcraft spirit. By speaking to these people, they might as well have been announcing their plans to all the demons around them because as soon as they speak to these people, the demons in the people will immediately report the plans to the next level of demons that handle destruction. The destructive demons will quickly attack the activity to sabotage or destroy it. **Most times, they will jump on the person that interviewed you and promised to give you the job while he or she is sleeping and turn the person's heart to disfavor you.** As a result, when you call with excitement to ask when you are to start the job, the person tells you that he or she has given the job to someone else and you are left wondering what happened.

If this has been the case in your life and depending on how critical what you are looking for is or how badly you want to succeed in life, you need to zip your lips about your plans and not share them with your friends or relatives. **My advice is to pray in tongues and let God open the door without**

informing the elements of sabotage around you. Unless you know that someone has no jealously, resentment or is not threatened by your impending success, you should never share your future plans with them. One thing among some so-called friends is that as long as everyone in the group is struggling with poverty, unmarriedness, unhappiness, etc., there are no threats. Trouble begins when one person within the group breaks through the ranks and jealousy develops. The jealousy becomes an invitation or an evil signal through anyone that carries the eavesdropping spirit in the group for the devils to come and sabotage the person's good prospect.

This is also one of the reasons why when some people become successful, they are shocked to find out that some of the people that they thought would be happy for them actually turn against them; even within their families. Jealousy is very evil because it sends an invitation to the devil for destruction. Therefore, you have to know who your friends really are because there are some 'unfriendly friends' out there. Know them and stay away from them. As you grow in the Lord, you will find out that there is an anointing to discern the spirits in people as well as people's thoughts. It helps to know who your friends really are. **Below is a narration of my encounters with someone who was a carrier of a monitoring spirit.** The Lord allowed me to discern what the spirit in him was saying to me:

My Encounters with 'Eavesdropping' & 'Monitoring' Spirits

The owner of a company where I was working at one time was a very self-absorbed guy with a Porsche and he basically thought that he was God's gift to women; he dressed the part. As far as I can tell, he had never been to a city in Africa or any remote African village. One day, I was coming out of the office building on my way to lunch and as I walked by his car, it seemed as if he was waiting for someone in his car by the front door of the building. To my surprise, the spirit in this man who I can tell will not be caught dead in a remote African village was singing a song of reproach against me in my dad's grandfather's old village language! I mean, the spirit went all the way back to the remote African village where my dad's grandfather's was born.

As a baby Christian, I was in shock and I did not know what to do as I stood there and looked at him. I wondered how his spirit knew the language that is spoken in my dad's grandfather's village. **I knew that the guy does not speak any African language but the spirit in him was singing fluently in the old language that we do not even speak because it is so old.** *I cannot even speak the language fluently. I walked away thinking that he was strange and I did not understand what had happened until one day when I met with someone about publishing their manuscript. I had to drive from the city of Lawrenceville in Gwinnett County to a place close to the Atlanta Airport for the meeting.*

When I was coming back, I decided to stop at a grocery store for some groceries and as I was getting out of my car, there was this guy coming out of the grocery store and walking towards his car that was parked next to mine. **As he was about to unlock his car, the spirit in him began to repeat verbatim the conversation that I had with the author of the manuscript over 30 miles away!** *The spirit was just quoting the things that we said to each other and it was then that <u>I realized that I had to deal with the spirit in my life from my bloodline</u>. I also became aware that I just had a meeting with someone that also carries a monitoring spirit. The first thing that I did was to bring my encounter with the author under the blood of Jesus so that the 'eavesdropping' spirit or "Peeping Tom" spirit cannot sabotage my publishing business. I then sought the Lord for my deliverance from the eavesdropping spirit. I needed the doors to the witchcraft spirit in my bloodline shut.*

I have since learned that spiritually, we all have to know who we are talking to because most people do not know that they carry these spirits or that the spirits are working against them. **I was one of them until the Lord began to teach me about them after He delivered me.** Because of the bloodline that is an 'open door' to the operation of these spirits, their carriers become instruments of sabotage in the hands of the devil without realizing it. I have seen some people who actually have a camera lens in one or both of their eyes and as you are talking to them or showing them something, the camera lens is rolling as its records what is going on or what is being said.

Whatever plans you share or show to them gets attacked because their recorded materials are reported to the next level of demons for destruction. As a result, they are the ones who tell the destructive demons about those around them that are trying to prosper so they can attack them. **You have to understand that the things that you see in the physical are just a tiny bit of what happens in the realm of the spirit because the realm of the spirit is vaster than the physical realm.**

Witchcraft and Worship of Ancestral Spirits

One major thing about the West African witchcraft is that it is rooted in pagan religions that **promote the worship of multiple-gods and the worship of ancestral spirits**. The **witchdoctors, priests and priestess** are credited with the ability to commune with the 'gods', good spirits and evil spirits. Many people hold the worship of their ancestral spirits in high regard. They solicit the help of the witchdoctors, priests or priestesses to help them consult the 'gods' or to help them appease the 'gods' when they believe that the 'gods' are angry with them or that 'gods' have afflicted them or their family members. These needs or circumstances that lead them to solicit help are usually because of unexplainable deaths, sicknesses, diseases or hardship.

As a result, a lot of communities have an ancestral or a local shrine at which they offer sacrifices to their dead ancestors or to the 'gods'. Lots of West African pagan events including traditional prayers, marriages, ceremonies or celebrations are usually started with the acknowledgement of the presence of the ancestors or the ancestral spirits and by giving them a 'drink offering' known as libation (pouring a drink on the ground). They will sometimes kill a goat or a chicken and pour the blood out to their ancestors on an iron or a stone. A proper sacrifice is then prepared with the meat of the animal as well as other types of food and they are placed at cross roads, by the banks of rivers, by trees or by their houses for the ancestral spirits.

In the West African culture, there has always been a need to be spiritual but due to the various pagan doctrines, what the people ended up with is the worship of idols. They were taught that the idols they worship were somehow connected to the main God who gave them specific jurisdictions over certain areas. **As a result, an average West African pagan believes in the One Main God but also in the lesser 'gods' that they think are connected to Him.** This belief led the people to begin the worship of the 'god of fire', 'god of iron', 'god of stone', 'water spirits', 'god of thunder', etc. They also believe in the power of their dead ancestors to protect and watch over them. **It is the reason why idol worship and ancestral worship are very common in West Africa and they are not viewed to be in conflict with the worship of the One Main God of the Bible.**

This is why as a missionary in Africa, you have to teach the people that once they are born again, they cannot lump their new Christian birth in Christ with the idols that they have been worshiping. They need to know about the difference between the God in the Bible and the idols that they call gods. I once had to rebuke a lady that I knew who after being 'born again', continued to worship the so-called 'god of iron'. She saw nothing wrong with it so I came down hard on her in my effort to get her to focus on the Lord and forsake pagan practices.

Hindrances by the Witchcraft Spirit

People that have witchcraft in their bloodline are caught in a lifelong battle in their attempt to move ahead in life. When they try to take one step forward, the witchcraft spirit fights to make them take several steps backwards. For example, when they save $1,000, they get a $2,500 problem. Also, when their income tax refund is on the way to them, their cars or major appliances suddenly go bad and require the entire tax refund plus some more money to repair them. These people are caught in a life cycle of 'going around the mountain' over and over again.

There are some that whenever they start a new business, it somehow manages to fail or get squashed and they do not know why. In other words, they are in a lifelong battle for a breakthrough that somehow seems to elude them. **What they are not aware of is the witchcraft door in their bloodline that is wide open for the spirits of destruction to come and go in their lives.** As a result, success and prosperity always mange to escape them. If the person is ignorant or does not want to deal with this evil spirit, the person will continue to leave him or herself open for the evil spirits to defeat. When the person dies, the spirits will move on to his or her children.

Covenants with the Witchcraft Spirit or Familiar Spirits

Our God is a God of covenants. Even when we make them with our enemies; He honors them because they prevent Him from intervening in the situation concerning us. He gave us a 'free will' or the ability to make choices for good or evil in our lives. **Man's encounter with the evil covenant began the day that Eve decided of her own 'free will' to have a taste of what evil was like in the Garden of Eden. Unfortunately, she could not say afterwards, "Oh, I tasted it and I do not**

like it; now, away evil." Instead, the devil laid claim to both Adam and Eve (they both ate) and all their descendants because they made an evil covenant with the devil by eating his fruit. **They chose to partake of evil and it is the reason that the world is full of evil today. The devil is the <u>Tree of Evil</u> and he became a part of humanity from then on; even from the womb** — Psalm 58:3:

> **"The wicked are <u>estranged from the womb</u>:** they go astray as soon as they be born, speaking lies."

It is the reason that you do not have to teach anyone evil, we were all born with it and hence we have to be taught to do good all the time. **The bad news is that everyone that is not yet 'born again' is still to this day, under the influence of the covenant that Adam made with the devil in the Garden of Eden to taste evil.** We all came from Adam and he made that decision for himself and for his descendants (us). Do you know how many years ago the covenant was made? Almost six thousand years ago! With this in mind, we can think about the recent covenants made on our behalf by our grandparents, parents and ourselves before coming to the Lord. We all have to be free from the evil covenants of the generations before us because they represent open doors for the devil and his agents to rise up against us.

Brotherhood of Jesus and Judas Iscariot

With the witchcraft spirit, the bloodline and family relationships matter a lot. The reason for this as we saw earlier in witchcraft **'death assignment', a family member of the intended victim is needed to betray the innocent victim.** A very good example that the Lord showed me was what happened between **Him** and **Judas Iscariot.** Throughout the Lord Jesus' ministry, the Jewish leaders could not touch Him; every time they came against Him, they could not harm Him because <u>He had no 'open door' for the devil to come through</u>. **That changed the very day that He cut a 'brotherhood**

covenant' with His disciples and Judas became His brother. It was not even up to an hour before Judas left to betray Him; the devil came through Judas against Him! Judas' greed and love of money attracted the devil and as soon as he became Jesus' brother through a covenant, just like the witches, he betrayed Jesus! Betrayal is a vital principal that the devil uses because he does not know love or loyalty.

As for the Lord Jesus, for the first time in His life (after the brotherhood covenant with His disciples including Judas), there was an 'open door' against Him called Judas and the devil went through it to get to Him. This shows us the power of relational covenants; the Lord Jesus became a brother to Judas Iscariot and to us all who believe in Him and it made Him vulnerable to the devil through Judas. Therefore, we need to know the covenants that have been made for and against us; especially if they were made with religious, familiar or witchcraft spirit way back in our bloodline.

We need to address these covenants and to renounce them in order to close the 'open doors' that they represent to the devil against us. For more information on covenants and their power, see my book titled: *Understanding the Power of Covenants.* I had to renounce a whole lot of evil covenants that were made against me by the generations before me. I especially had to renounce the witchcraft covenants because of the activities of my dad's maternal grandfather who was a witchdoctor. **You will notice that I am using the terms "my dad's mother" instead of "my grandmother," and "my dad's father" instead of "my grandfather" so that I do not reopen the doors that they had represented against me by their witchcraft activities.** I am now a **new creation** in Christ Jesus and I want it to stay that way.

The Life of My Dad's Maternal Grandfather — a Witchdoctor

My dad's mother believed that her dad used his witchcraft power as a witchdoctor to do good things for people and to save lives. One of such occasions was the story concerning her own birth. She told me that her dad pleaded with the witches to spare her life when her mother was pregnant with her and the witches wanted to kill her. **According to her, her dad was a very powerful witchdoctor to the kings and was revered throughout his life time.** As part of his profession, he would attend witches' nighttime gatherings to negotiate terms for his clients and to make bargains with them to stay away from harming them. Below is one such example:

She told me that her dad used his witchcraft power to save the life of her eldest son. All I knew as I was growing up was that her eldest son (my father's eldest brother) had one leg and he also had scars of what may have once been some serious blotches or boils all over his skin. *One day, she decided to tell me how her eldest son lost his leg and how her dad used his witchcraft powers to save his life.* She said that her husband (my dad's father) had a quarrel with his neighbor over a piece of land and the neighbor in anger said to him, "You will see;" a witchcraft term for WAR. A few days later, her eldest son and his brothers went to the farm and he was bitten by a snake. The farm was far from town so by the time they made it home, the venom had destroyed the leg and it had to be amputated. *According to her, what she was not aware of at the time was that the neighbor actually wanted the life of her son.* As a wizard, the neighbor had received the support of another witch in her husband's family and they had already launched a 'death assignment' against her eldest son. Her dad lived in another city and was not aware of this evil plan.

In line with the assignment, the witches gathered together on a certain night, killed, boiled and ate her eldest son before her dad found out that such an assignment had been carried out against one of his grandsons and he was furious. *Knowing that the events are yet to manifest in the physical, he went to the witches' nightly meeting and in his anger, commanded every witch to vomit every part of his grandson that they had boiled and eaten. They all did but the two that ate the leg had died and as a result, her son only lost a leg but his life was saved. Due to the fact that it was a 'death assignment' that was sent against him, he also came down with a sickness that left blotches on his skin which she said was because the witches had actually boiled his flesh before eating him. She said that the scars are the evidence of what they had done to him but she was glad her dad saved his life.*

The Last Day of My Dad's Maternal Grandfather

Witchdoctors work with the aid of familiar spirits but at the end, these demons destroy them. In other words, the evil spirits usually make sure that the very people that they had used as their mediums, carriers or agents go to hell at the end of their lives. **A good example of this was the story that my dad's mother told me about how her dad died.** <u>I never met him but it is a story that I hope will open the eyes of all those who are currently involved in witchcraft or use the aids of familiar spirits</u>. To her, the story was a demonstration of her dad's triumphant entry into heaven but to me, it was the story of a great deception:

She said that on her dad's death bed and at the point his death, he sent her to get a bucket of water and a towel as he was directed by the spirits that had been working through him as a witchdoctor. He told her that the spirits showed him a so-called 'mountain leading into heaven' and they told him that he was about to die. **They also told him that he was "about to ascend the mountain to enter into heaven" and that as a result, he was in "for a long climb into heaven!"** *According to her, she watched as he was covered with sweat and as he kept on 'climbing the mountain' that she could not see. As he climbed, the sweat became too much and she began wiping him off with the towel that she had dipped in the bucket of water.*

She watched as he panted and sweated in his response to the spirits' instruction to "climb up higher." He kept on climbing until finally, he died of exhaustion. That was how my dad's maternal grandfather died while responding to the instructions of the evil spirits that he had worked with to "climb up higher." **He died believing that he was climbing this invisible mountain into heaven. Instead, he was deceived by the evil spirits and their tactic was to make him wear his heart out because he was an old man.**

The truth is that he was not a Christian so, where do you think the spirits dragged him to? At the time that my dad's mother told me this story, I too did not know that he did not climb into heaven. I also did not know that he was not serving God by being a 'good wizard' (male witch). **As for my dad's mother, she was proud of the gallant way that her dad left this earth and entered into heaven.** She believed that the spirits that worked through him while he was alive helped him to climb into heaven! **I only realized that my dad's maternal grandfather was destroyed by demons when I became 'born again'.** The evil spirits gave him the illusion that he was climbing into heaven; someplace good. **As a result, he used all his strength to climb up higher on some mountain that he believed was leading into heaven and he died doing it.**

Knowing how the devil operates, I also now realize that at the end his life, those demons had a field day mocking and laughing at him for believing their false report that he was climbing into heaven. Yes, they later ridiculed him for having been a fool. It makes me furious when I think of how this man wasted his life in serving demons and how they led him straight to hell. **My dad's maternal grandfather was not alone in the delusion that working with the aids of familiar spirit is a godly venture.** All those who serve the devil have the same fate. He does not have a single good plan for anyone that choose him instead of God. The devil and his demons want to make everyone's fate like their fate — suitable only for destruction. This is why the Lord Jesus wanted us to know in **John 10:10** that:

> "The thief cometh not, but for **to steal**, and **to kill, and to destroy: I am come that they might have life, and that they might have it more abundantly.**"

The Lord Jesus is the only way into heaven and no one has to climb some mountain into heaven but only believe in Jesus and His works. This is why He said in **John 14:6:**

> "… I am the way, the truth, and the life: **no man cometh unto the Father, but by me.**"

Healing 'Powers' of Witchdoctors

You can only find life in Christ through the Holy Spirit; no other spirit that is talking to you through a witchdoctor or a medium is of God. **In West Africa, the demons use the spirit of infirmities to play tic-tac-toe with people.** For instance, when a person goes to see a witchdoctor for a headache, the witchdoctor will do incantations for the person or give him or her something to drink. The headache will go away and but soon after, the person returns with another type of ailment because what the demons did was to back off from the headache and gave the person a new sickness like a foot or stomach pain. When the person gets 'healed' of the foot and stomach pain, his or her back will begin to give them problems because the demons want to keep the person going to the witchdoctor all the time.

In other words, just when they think that they are getting better and that everything is going well with them, the demons inject them with something new to bring them right back to the witchdoctor's house. It is a form of patronage and worship. **When the person runs out of reasons to go to the witchdoctor, the person is then told to pray so that his or her child who lives away from home is not brought back in a casket.** Now, the witchdoctor really has the person panicking.

This is one of the reasons why some of the witchdoctors live like kings because people give them cars and houses. The people truly believe that the witchdoctors are successfully 'curing' them of various sicknesses and diseases because they never get the understanding that the witchdoctors are recycling infirmities in their bodies.

Witchcraft spirit also launch a 'recycling of infirmities' assignment against many people in this country. As a result, there are people who constantly go in and out of the hospital with one sickness after another. Just when they think that they are finally over a certain sickness and they speak with someone who carries the spirit of infirmities, they come down with a new one. Sometimes, the people themselves are the carriers of the spirits of infirmities that were passed down to them from the previous generations. If this has been your story, recognize it as an assignment by the witchcraft spirit and say NO to it. Seek the Lord to deliver you from it because it is not His portion for you.

The Aid of Familiar Spirits in Modern Society

As I stated earlier, witchcraft is not just being stubborn, rebellious or practicing iniquity and as you have read so far, it is deeper than these things. A true witch uses the aid of familiar spirits that endue him or her with some kind of supernatural power or knowledge to do some things that they cannot do in their own strength. In modern society, **these spirits will use people dressed in glamorous clothes as their vessels to mislead young people and to model debauchery lifestyles with the promise of some type of prosperity**. Their victims never really prosper in any good way because the money they make leads them to premature deaths from drug overdose or accidents. They are destroyed by the very things the devil gave them. They fulfill what is written in **Proverbs 1:32:**

"For the turning away of the simple shall slay them, and **the prosperity of fools shall destroy them.**"

You have heard testimonies of people in the music or entertainment business that the devil promised fame and fortune if they would just hand over their souls to him. In other words, the devil promised them fame and fortune in exchange for their souls! Those who are ignorant of the Word of God and the value of their human soul, enter into the evil covenant with the devil and his familiar spirits. In doing this, they sign over their souls to the devil for all of eternity for a few years of fame and fortune. They do not realize that their souls are more precious than all the fame, gold and silver in the whole world. The devil and his evil spirits deceive the people with the lure of power or fame. I told you about the end of my dad's maternal grandfather's life and how those demons deceived him to believe that he was ascending to heaven and how he 'climbed' some invisible mountain till he died.

Familiar Spirits Appearing in Visions and Dreams

Familiar spirits like to make contact with people through visions and dreams. They might pretend to be your <u>dead relative</u> in order to gain access into your life. The minute you accept the familiar spirit as being your relative that passed away who is now visiting or talking to you in visions or dreams, you open the door against yourself to them. When this happens, in due time, you will begin to suffer from the very medical or financial conditions that the dead relative suffered from before he or she died. Make no mistake about their intentions because the only reason they are coming to you is to make your body their new 'host body' since they lost their previous 'host body' — your dead relative!

As a result, you have to be careful not to let them into your life because those who allow them into their lives get destroyed by them through sicknesses and diseases. For more understanding on this, see 2 of my books titled, *'Keys to Understanding Your Visions and Dreams'* and *'How to Discern and Expel Evil Spirits'*.

My Victory over the Witchcraft Spirit of 'Mind Control'

Before I tell you what happened to me, I want to let you know that <u>there are people out there in the world who use the witchcraft spirit of 'mind control' and 'thoughts projection' to program people to do their will</u>. Some men and women use it to get a person to fall in love with them and to make the person become addicted to them. This is one of the reasons why some ladies cannot get rid of a boyfriend that treats them very badly. They keep trying but are not able to get away because they get reprogramed by the boyfriend. **There are those who use 'mind control' through some mystic rituals or astral projection to move objects as well as to send their thoughts to people.** Make no mistake about it, they are all a form of witchcraft. Below are my encounters with a couple of them:

*Some time ago, we were out on evangelism and we were witnessing to people at the Centennial Park in Atlanta. I wanted to witness to a guy that I thought was a homeless person who was lying on a bench at the Park. I was getting tired so I decided to sit on the bench across from the guy and rest a while. **My plan was to walk over to him when I get up but I was shocked when he looked at me and he immediately began sending me thoughts in his attempt to program me to do his will; he was trying to control me with his mind!** To me, I knew that he was in for a rude awaking because I had the same experience once before in Africa with a guy on a bus that also tried to program me and to control me with his mind.*

*During the encounter with the first guy on the bus, the Lord taught me how to overcome the witchcraft spirit of **mind control**. It was a weird experience because as soon as I sat down on the bus, the guy sitting across from me began to speak to me through his thoughts saying that he wanted me to focus on him and to begin to desire him above everything else. **He wanted me to believe that I cannot live without him and I almost jumped up from my seat but the Lord told*** *me not to be afraid but to begin meditating on Psalm 23.* *Knowing that the Lord was present with me, I looked the guy squarely in the face and I began to recite Psalm 23 in my heart. I was amazed at the power of the Word of God because without realizing that I was meditating on the Word of God, the guy became furious as he began asking me through his thoughts if I heard what he said. I watched him as the Word of God cut him like a knife as he was again sending me the thoughts! He jumped up from his seat and I laughed as I continued to recite Psalm 23 in my heart.*

Based on this past experience, I also looked at the guy on the bench squarely in the eye and I began to recite Psalm 23 in my heart and he got up. He looked at me and was furious so I got up and walked over to him on the bench. Before I could open my mouth, he said, "Excuse me, what power do you have?" I replied in anger, "What power do you think that you have in trying to program me? My power is greater than yours." He said, "I know and that is why I am asking you, what power do you have?" I said, "I have the power of the blood of Jesus and the Word of God and it cuts like a knife." He reached into his chest and underneath his shirt and pulled out a talisman that he had on his neck. He raised it up and he dropped it to the ground saying, "I do not want this anymore because no power has ever been able to counteract or defeat its power but today, you broke it."

He told me that he traveled to India to get the power in the talisman and that he went through initiations and rituals to get the power. **I told him that he needed to get the real power that is from God and he did not need to go to India.** *Needless to say that I led him to the Lord and he told members of my group what happened between us and how what he thought was power was not real power and they were shocked. I told everyone that first, we had our battle in the realm of the spirit, then it was brought down to the physical realm and now he has seen that Jesus has the greater power.*

As you can see in my encounter with both guys, none of them could harm me because I am a **'born again'** Christian! This is why I tell Christians to never be afraid of anyone who claims to be a witch or a wizard because they cannot harm us. As a **'born again'** Christians, the Word of God says in **Colossians 3:3** that we are dead and our lives are hid with Christ in God. Therefore, no witch or wizard can get to us:

> "**For ye are dead, and <u>your life is hid with Christ in God</u>.**"

No witch or wizard can pass through Christ to get to us in God. It is one of the reasons that the Lord said to us — fear not!

Chapter 7
The Voodoo Type of Witchcraft

What is Voodoo?

Voodoo is also spelled as Vodun, Voudou and in French as Vaudou. In the Fon language of the Republic of Benin (formerly Dahomey) the word Vodou means 'spirit' or 'deity'. The voodoo tradition includes all walks of life in the Republic of Benin, Congo, Yoruba in Nigeria and Haiti. **It involves not just religion but justice, philosophy, medicine in which the practitioners believe that everything is spirit.** To them, human beings are spirits that dwell in the visible world while the invisible world is inhabited by ancestral spirits (iwa), angels (zanj), mysteries (myste) and those who recently passed away. They have priests and priestesses of various rankings.

The Origin of Voodoo

Voodoo began outside of Africa as a **'conglomeration' of the West African religious practices that different slaves brought with them to the Caribbean and parts of the Americas.** Meaning that the slaves that came from West African countries of Benin (formerly known as Dahomey), Congo and the Yoruba tribe of Nigeria essentially "creolized" the religious practices from their native lands that they brought with them as slaves. **In the 16th and 17th centuries, the Roman Catholic missionaries 'Christianized' voodoo as a form of religion in what was formerly known as <u>Saint-Domingue</u> but now known as <u>Haiti</u>.**

Today, voodoo is now closely associated with Haiti and regions that have been under French influence or have French connections such as the Louisiana area of the United States. **Together with Roman Catholicism, voodoo is the official religion of Haiti.** This is not surprising since voodoo and Catholicism are mixed in Haiti. It was actually a Roman

Catholic Priest (Jean-Bertrand Aristide) that declared voodoo the official religion of Haiti when he became President.

Those who promote the practice of voodoo in Haiti think that they are affirming their African roots without realizing that they are making themselves abominable to God. God hates idolatry and witchcraft in Africa and everywhere else. There is a great need to evangelize this group in Haiti.

The Goal of Voodoo Practitioners

The main objective of the voodoo practitioners is to serve the spirits and in return, the spirits will give them good health, favor, prosperity and protection. As a result, they beat the drum and dance at their ceremonies in order to invite the spirits to come and possess them. **Spiritual possession is a vital aspect of their ceremony as they eat and drink so that they can enter into a trance as the spirits possess them.** The 'ancestral spirits' make them mediums and transform them into 'supernatural human beings' that are able to do things that defy normal human abilities. We know that this is nothing but the works of demons.

Among the Yoruba tribes of Nigeria, these spirits are called 'eyo' and they are worshipped by dressing up as masquerades. Those who will serve as masquerades spend a great deal of time performing secret rituals for months so that they can be totally possessed or inhabited by the spirits on the day that they come out to celebrate these spirits. **The voodoo practitioners believe that when these masquerades come out, the people wearing the full body masks are the incarnate of the spirit that entered them. In other words, they believe that the men wearing the <u>full body masquerade gears</u> are not humans but gods!** On the day of their national celebration, these masquerades that have become possessed by the evil spirits take over the streets of Lagos in Nigeria and a lot of the Yoruba people truly regard them as 'gods'.

Due to this belief, humans are not supposed to look at them in the eye or be on the same street with them on the day of their national celebration. They are very fierce and truly mean as they carry whips with which they will mercilessly beat anyone that does not run when they see them coming. To me, they are very demonic. I have personally seen a person that was possessed by one of these spirits in Lagos perform amazing feats as they move at lightning speed! I watched as one of them entered a street and when he leaped, he was almost at the end of the street which was an impossible task for a normal person. In my book titled, **Experiencing the Depths of the Holy Spirit;** *Pages 176-177*, I talked about my encounter with one of these masquerades and how the Lord Holy Spirit protected me from being beaten by him. Below is an excerpt:

"Some years ago, I went home at the time that they were having an 'Eyo; Masquerade Day' in Lagos, Nigeria and I was not aware of it. The original inhabitants of Lagos believed that these masquerades are 'gods' and humans are not to come into contact with them on the streets. Therefore, on the day that these masquerades come out, most people stay off the streets or wait for them to vacate the streets before going out on foot. Some people get in their cars and wind up their car windows because if you wind down your window, these masquerades carry whips made of cowhide and they will whip you mercilessly for daring to confront a 'god' on the street in a car with an open window.

The men that wear these masquerade masks totally give themselves over to demons and they can take one step from a very far distance and the next thing you know they are right there in front of you with a demonic speed. Because I now live in the USA, I had forgotten about this evil day in Lagos and on this day, I did not pay attention to the fact that the street looked deserted. I had a guest and I had walked with the guest to the bus stop but on my way back, I found myself face to face with two of these masquerades. One of them leaped out from nowhere and looked at me with an 'how dare you' type pose.

*I remember looking at him thinking, oh my God, I do not want these masquerades to mark me up with their whips because they will whip a person and put a permanent mark on the person's face. I have a cousin that was beaten by them years ago on his way back from the hospital and they left him with a permanent marked on his face. Therefore, as soon as he looked at me and was getting ready to charge at me, the **Holy Spirit** rose up inside of me and said, 'If he comes near you, he is a dead man.' <u>I knew it was a sovereign decree from Almighty God so, I stood firm with my hands on my hips</u>! You should have seen it; I stood and said in my heart that I was not moving. I stood firmly and he took a look at me for a while and he ran off in the opposite direction." Praise the Lord for keeping us."*

The Role of the Serpent in Voodoo Practice

Voodoo practice is very closely associated with the worship of the serpent. For the voodoo priests and priestesses, the serpent has a very high or elevated place in their rituals and beliefs. It is regarded as their gatekeeper between man on earth and God in heaven. **They believe that a snake with its tail in its mouth represents the circle of infinity; the sign of the rainbow that God left on earth for man!** To them, <u>the serpent also gives them a connection to God, the knowledge of the ancient world and a connection to their ancestors</u>. The serpent is their wisdom giver, their provider and their fusion of two becoming one; it is their transformation enabler because their belief is that God left it as the rainbow (infinity) on earth with man. As a Christian, you can see that the devil sold them a lie from the pit of hell concerning God and the serpent.

According to some writers, the word voodoo now essentially means "the snake under whose supervision guides all those who share the voodoo faith." **For example, there is a certian town in Nigeria where the people claim that a particular snake is the 'mother of the town'!** As a result, they worship and reverence this snake. Although the practice was no longer common when I was growing up, I remember the day that someone got into trouble for killing this particular type of snake. It was this incident that highlighted and made the practice of worshipping a snake memorable to me because it was a very strange incident.

In a lot of West African communities, people used to sleep outside because it gets very hot and they did not have air conditioning**. It was not uncommon to sleep outside in the open air or to leave your doors and windows open both day and night.** This particular snake that they worship and call their 'mother' likes the smell of newborn babies. According to them, if you leave a new born baby unattended in the farm or at home, this snake will come into the tent or house and coil itself up as a pillow under the baby's head. It does not bite or hurt the baby but it is attracted to the smell and warmth of newborn babies. As a result, mothers began to treat this particular type of snake like a babysitter or one who keeps their babies when they are not there.

In due time, people began to reverence and regard this snake as a mother! **When they find this snake under the baby's head, they do not kill it but lift the baby up and let the snake crawl away. <u>As the snake is crawling away, they would begin to praise and thank it for watching over the baby.</u>** It became a taboo to kill this particular type of snake. This was the snake that someone that I knew killed and got in trouble for. He came home one day and saw a snake underneath the head of his new born baby and he removed the baby but took a machete and wacked the snake to pieces. Some people in the town made a big deal out of it because he had done something that was forbidden. **They regarded his killing of the snake as equivalent to the killing of a human being and they wanted him to give the snake a burial befitting a human being.** Because he was a Muslim, he refused to give a serpent any kind of burial so there was commotion.

Voodoo Rituals

In voodoo rituals, the high priests or the high priestesses are the medium through which the serpent expresses its power. This is why they dance with a serpent around their neck or in their midst during their rituals. In other words, those who practice voodoo center many of their activities around the serpent as they believe that it gives them certain powers, knowledge, connection to their ancestors and connection to God. They will even make serpent dolls out of Spanish moss, yarn, cloth and ribbons to represent the serpent when they have no live serpent for their rituals.

Also, they believe that the serpent moves through them to perform cures, cast spells or charms as they yield their bodies up for possession by the serpentine spirit. To us who know the Bible, we can clearly see that the voodoo worshippers of the serpent are seriously misinformed about what the devil did to Adam and Eve and to all of humanity through the serpent. **Therefore, voodoo is a misguided practice borne out of pure lies by an evil spirit; the same spirit that lied to Eve in the Garden of Eden.** The truth is that the serpent has never done anything good and it never will because it has been cursed by God forever as we see in **Genesis 3:14-15:**

> "And the LORD God said unto the serpent, Because thou hast done this, **thou art cursed above all cattle, and above every beast of the field; upon thy belly shalt thou go, and dust shalt thou eat all the days of thy life**: 15 And I will **put enmity** between thee and the woman, and between thy seed and her seed; it shall bruise thy head, and thou shalt bruise his heel."

As you can see, the serpent is forever cursed by God and there is no love lost between man and the serpent because God has put enmity between us and the serpent forever! Therefore, those who worship the serpent are lost and they are clueless concerning God and His Word in the Bible.

The Wicked Activities of the Voodoo Priests and Priestesses

Besides their religious activities, voodoo priests and priestesses claim to have supernatural abilities to cast spells, to charm and to enchant people for a fee. Some of their activities involve the use of dolls (representation of the person they are trying to harm). Those who practice voodoo make many claims and some of them even give a 'money back guarantee' for those who will solicit their evil services. They boast of their abilities to:

- Perform cures or heal people
- Cast spells
- Break up relationships, heal relationships
- Kill your enemies for you
- Charm the person you want to have a relationship with
- Bring people back from the dead
- Enhance sexual abilities
- Help you harm or get rid of those who are jealous or envious of you
- Help you get wealth or charm someone to turn over their wealth to you and so forth

'Blanking Out' Someone's Mind

To 'blank out' someone's mind means to make a person suffer a temporary loss of his or her senses (loss of common sense) so that he or she is stupid enough to obey any command the voodoo practitioners or their clients issue to the person. In other words, voodoo priests and priestesses believe that they have the ability to cast a particular spell to 'blank out' people's minds so that you can make them do whatever you want them to do. **For example, they boast of the ability to give someone a charm so when they shake hands with a stranger, they can command the stranger to turn over everything valuable in his or her pocket, wallet or handbag and the stranger will obey.** By the time the victim regains his or her senses, the person that they shook hands with is long gone.

These things are not figments of people's imaginations because while I was growing up, I heard many accounts from people who went to the market with some money and after their encounter with a stranger through a handshake or conversation, they could not account for how their money vanished from their pocket or wallet! It is a way of robbing people with the aid of voodoo instead of a gun. **There are those who kidnap people, kill and keep the dead (embalmed) body in a secret place in their homes so that when commanded, the dead body vomits out money. They believe that it is even more profitable if it is a pregnant woman at the time she was abducted.** This is reportedly a well-known practice in some parts of Nigeria where some men have been suspected of using people in this manner to enrich themselves. As I stated before, the voodoo practitioners are totally given over to the worship of the devil and in return, he gives them evil power to practice these types of wickedness.

Again, you will come across those who claim to use their voodoo powers for good but do not believe them because nothing good can come out of the devil. **To a 'born again' Christian, their power is of no effect because of the blood of Jesus. All we have to do is plead the blood of Jesus and their power becomes null and void!** As a result, I feel sorry for any agent of the devil who makes claims of being able to perform cures, use people for money or send charms against people because I know that all that the devil is using the person to do is spread his wickedness and <u>at the end, he destroys them</u>. Do not be deceived by their claims of abilities to heal because, we know that true and lasting healing comes from the Lord Jesus Christ and as for casting spells, <u>it is written concerning us</u> in **Isaiah 54:17** that:

> **"No weapon that is formed against thee shall prosper; and every tongue that shall rise against thee in judgment thou shalt condemn.** This is the heritage of the servants of the LORD, and their righteousness is of me, saith the LORD."

Therefore, no voodoo practitioner shall be able to harm us as we walk in righteousness and avoid fraternizing with them. Do not be afraid of any evil spirit because you have more power than them.

Use of Sorcery and Divination

The West African witchdoctors and the voodoo priests and priestesses practice sorcery and divination with the aid of familiar spirits. Many people go to them on a regular basis to divine for them concerning problems they are having. **Sorcery involves the use of items such as hair, clothing and other personal belongings to carry out the divination or enchantments and curses against the person.** In other words, a person's personal items like a dress or underwear can be used to harm the person by casting spells and pronouncing curses on them. The voodoo priests and priestesses yield themselves to the powers of evil spirits who then direct them in the process of divination and spell casting on how to destroy the person.

In divination, the familiar spirits use them to carry out 'acts of foretelling future events or revealing occultic knowledge'. The spirits also help them to bewitch, enchant, and conjure up wicked assignments on behalf of those requesting their evil services. They help these people to destroy or hinder anyone that they regard as their enemy or as the source of their problems.

For example, when a person visits a witchdoctor or voodoo priest, they will announce the devil's plan to the person such as, **"Someone in the person's family is going to die in 2 months if the person does not bring a sacrifice to the idol that the person worships."** If the person fails to bring the sacrifice and someone dies in his or her family, the person then begins to believe that the prediction by the witchdoctor was accurate. **What the person was not aware of was that the devil targeted to kill someone in his or her family all along** and by accepting or believing the words of the witchdoctor, the person actually aided the devil in killing the person who died in his or her family by having faith in the words of the devil!

The Difference between West African Witchcraft and Voodoo

As we have already seen, both voodoo priests, priestesses and witchdoctors use familiar spirits to engage in divinations and soothsaying. It is by the power of familiar spirits that they cast spells and use charms against unsuspecting people. **The major difference between voodoo practice and the original West African witchcraft is that many of the voodoo 'practitioners'** do not possess the ability to fly at night. Some of their members who are also witchdoctors, witches and wizards may possess the ability to fly but the regular members cannot fly at night. In other words, the ordinary voodoo members cannot eject their souls into animals like cats, birds, dogs or even flies. This is a great difference when it comes to abilities in the hierarchy of wickedness.

As a result, the wicked activities by regular voodoo members are usually practiced on the natural level with physical objects; they are not first plotted and carried out in the spiritual realm. **In other words, those who practice voodoo and cast spells do not have the ability to fly in the nighttime to a wicked gathering but they can plot evil against people with the aid of wicked spirits during the day.** Although they do not fly, they actually meet on a regular basis for their evil activities so we cannot underestimate their influence.

The Only True Protection against Voodoo

Becoming a 'born again' Christian is the only true protection against voodoo and all other forms of witchcrafts but you must renounce the covenant with the voodoo spirit as soon as you become 'born again'. What this means is that as a 'born again' Christian, if you or your spouse have voodoo in your bloodline, you cannot ignore it and say that because you are now 'born again', the voodoo covenant is automatically gone. You have to personally renounce the covenant with the voodoo spirit and replace it with the New Covenant that you now have with the Lord Jesus. **The reason for this is because your new birth does not automatically erase all the evil covenants that you and the generations before you made with the devil.**

Rather, your new birth means that your human spirit was recreated in Christ Jesus and that the Holy Spirit now dwells in your human spirit but it is your responsibility to renounce all the evil covenants that have been in your life. It is also your responsibility to renew your mind with the Word of God and to keep your body holy. God is not going to do these things for anyone of us. Therefore, it is our duty as Christians to defeat the devil (enforce the Lord's victory over him) in areas that the generations before us opened the doors in our bloodline for him to make our lives miserable. We are told in the Word of God that all things are ours but look at many of us; do we walk, look and act like people that have all things right now?

> "Therefore let no man glory in men. **For all things are yours;** 22 Whether Paul, or Apollos, or Cephas, **or the world, or life, or death, or things present, or things to come; all are yours;** 23 And ye are Christ's; and Christ is God's" (1 Corinthians 3:21-23).

What a lot of people do not realize is that there are demonic forces such as the voodoo spirits (one form of witchcraft) that are out to wrestle with us in their attempts to stop our blessings from coming forth in our lives. It is our responsibility to drive them out of our lives.

Chapter 8
Santeria as a Form of Witchcraft

Origin of Santeria

Santeria is a type of witchcraft practice that came from a combination of religions. These religions come from the Yoruba tribe of West Africa, pagan religions in the Caribbean, some Native Indian rituals and aspects of Roman Catholicism. Slaves imported from West Africa to the Caribbean (the New World) to work the sugarcane plantations carried with them various religious traditions from their old world into their New World in the Caribbean. They created **a system of worship** that **fused** some of their Yoruba religions, some Caribbean religions and some Native Indian rituals with aspects of Catholicism from the Roman Catholic Church.

Its origin in this regard is similar to voodoo. In light of this knowledge, you can safely say that Santeria is a potpourri of different pagan religious practices introduced by slaves from West Africa fused with Catholicism. As a result of being mixed with Catholicism, Santeria may seem normal or look like Roman Catholic rituals with some variation but make no mistake about the fact that it is pagan and it is demonic.

The Slaves' Attempts to Deceive Their Masters

The slaves introduced aspects of Catholicism into their rituals in their attempts to deceive their slave masters as to the true nature of their pagan religions. **They tried to make their rituals look as if they were Roman Catholic Church based. As a result, when the slave masters came to observe their ceremonies that involved chanting, drumming, gyrating, and going into trances, they were not able to discern the true nature of what the slaves were really practicing.** Part of the plan to deceive their masters involved giving the names of Christian saints to their pagan festivities. They began to center their religious ceremonies and rituals on saints supported by the Roman Catholic Church.

The Essence of Santeria

At its core, Santeria involves the practice of divination, the ceremonial beating of drums, dancing to induce trance and communication with ancestral spirits or deities. It also involves blood sacrifice using animals. They have priests that function as **diviners** of the **Orishas** (father of men). Originally, the **Ifá** (ee-fah) priests are considered to be highest in rank within **Santeria's** all-male group but now, women are serving as priestesses as well. The **Ifá** priests or priestesses are said to be the mouth-piece of the **Orisha** of prophecy, wisdom and knowledge. **Ifá** Priests are known by the title **Babalawo** or 'Father Who Knows the Secrets or **witchdoctor'.**

In West Africa, a lot of the witchdoctors (Babalawos) are also wizards in the traditional form of witchcraft and they provide divination services for fees. They can also send spells but all the practitioners believe in being bodily possessed by ancestral spirits or pagan gods. As a result, Santeria is just a modified form of the witchcraft practice in West Africa. It is to be considered dangerous to all who get involved in it.

Santeria's Influence in Cuba

Today, Santeria is practiced in many <u>Hispanic countries</u> such as **Puerto Rico, Cuba** and the **Dominican Republic.** Although Cuba is officially a Roman Catholic nation, Santeria is widely recognized and accepted as a valid form of religious worship along with Catholicism. It has the largest group of followers in Cuba and those who practice it are not ashamed of it but as 'born again' Christians, we must always remember that Santeria is nothing but a pagan religion disguised with Roman Catholic rituals. **It practitioners speak with ancestral spirits, engage in divination and use witchdoctors.** Nothing can be more witchcraft than this.

Santeria is one of the roots of generational curses among people from Cuba, Brazil and Puerto Rico but if you are 'born again', you do not have to fear that it can hurt you.

When you determine that you have Santeria practice in your bloodline, all you have to do is renounce every covenant that was made with it on your behalf by the generations before you so that the door to Santeria curses can be shut in your life. Afterwards, just ask God to forgive you in Jesus' name.

Santeria's Influence in the United States

Some time ago while evangelizing in the park at the Little Five Points in Atlanta, we ran into some Santeria practitioners. The men were beating the drums while the ladies were dancing to the drum beats and gyrating in their attempts to go into trances as a result of being bodily possessed by the 'spirits'. I watched as they were trying so hard to become possessed that they were totally abandoning themselves to the spirits. It was sad to watch them working so hard to get possessed when all they had to do is accept the Lord Jesus and receive TRUE POWER.

According to 2001 statistical records, there were an estimated 22,000 Santeria practitioners in the U.S. alone. Now, U.S. practitioners are estimated to be in the hundreds of thousands. From a Christian perspective, these are thousands of lost souls. In a word, we can say that Santeria is just like any other form of pagan religion that uses forms of witchcraft such as:

- Soothsaying
- Divination
- Devil worship
- Animal sacrifices
- Chanting and drumming to invite evil sprits
- Going into a trance with wild gyrations
- Demonic possession

The Quest for Power and Knowledge

Many people seek power and 'supernatural knowledge' from demonic sources instead of the Holy Spirit. **These people fall into different forms of witchcrafts because the**

devil uses their evil search to steer them to himself. His goal is to make himself available to them so that he can continue to deceive them concerning the 'power' that they think they have. From what you have read so far in this book, you can see that there is no such thing as an innocent association with the devil. **For example, during one of my teaching sessions, a lady gave an account of how her sister was drawn to 'strange books' and 'strange knowledge' and she became involved in Santeria. Eventually, she wound up in the psychiatric hospital because the devils began to vex her in the mind.**

According to her sister, she still likes her involvement in Santeria and would not give it up. The vexing of her mind by the devils is easy to understand because all they did was to begin to <u>make a withdrawal</u> from the 'strange knowledge' that they had deposited in her mind; her mind now belongs to them. There is an Africa saying that, "Every day for the thief but one day for the owner of the house." **This lady had 'good times' with the devil in her mind until the day came for her to pay up.** The sad part of this type of situation is that <u>unless she is willing to receive help from the Lord Jesus by giving up Santeria</u>, there is no way to help her or get her delivered from the occultic or witchcraft spirit that are vexing her.

As much as her sister loves her, we could not override her will; so as long as she is not willing to give up Santeria. Her sister can only pray for the Lord to touch her so that her ears will be open to receive the Word of God that brings salvation. Otherwise, if you pray against her will and try to lay hands on her, you might get attacked by the spirits because she wanted and invited them; **she has a covenant with them to make her mind their home.** The Lord taught me from the beginning that a person has a right to keep his or her demons and to go to hell if that is what the person wants. Therefore, be careful what you invite into your life. **The Lord does not override a person's will and neither should we.**

The Witchcraft Prayer of 'Binding People to God's Will'

Some years ago, there was a minister whose name I will not mention but she was preaching that believers should 'bind people to the will of God' as a way of getting people saved. **She said all you have to do is 'bind your relatives to the mind of Christ and to the will of God and they will begin to act accordingly'.** Initially, I did not recognize it as a form of witchcraft until the Lord showed it to me. **The Lord told me that 'binding people to His will' is a witchcraft prayer because He wants people to be loose from all that bind them and for those that love Him to come to Him of their own free will!** He does not want those who want nothing to do with Him to be 'bound to His will'. In other words, <u>the Lord wants people to be free to choose and not to be bound by another person's choice for them</u>. It is witchcraft to do so. Remember that the witchcraft spirit is passed onto unsuspecting victims through food and that the devil overrides their will? Well, our God does not operate that way. He wants you to choose life or death of your own free will.

According to Him, love is something that you cannot force someone to give you and you cannot buy. When you look at society at large, you will see people trying to use money to entice other people to love them or stay with them but at the end what happens? They lose in their game of trying to buy love. **Binding a person's will is a form of forcing the person to do your will.** <u>You cannot buy love or force a person to love you or love God. This is why God said that you have to come to Him of your own free will without anyone binding you to Him</u>! **He freely gives us His love and He wants us to freely reciprocate.** As a result, when I minister, I do not touch anyone that does not want hands laid on them or pray for someone to receive deliverance who does not want it.

Just take a minute to think about it; if 'binding people to His will' was God's way of getting people saved, God would have just waved His hand for all of us to be 'bound to His will' and we will all become 'born again' and the whole world would be saved! We are told in **1 Corinthians 1:21-25** that **God chose the preaching of the Gospel which some people regard as foolishness as a way to get people saved:**

"For after that in the wisdom of God the world by wisdom knew not God, **it pleased God by the foolishness of preaching to save them that believe.** 22 For the Jews require a sign, and the Greeks seek after wisdom: 23 But we preach Christ crucified, unto the Jews a stumblingblock, and unto the Greeks foolishness; 24 But unto them which are called, both Jews and Greeks, Christ the power of God, and the wisdom of God. 25 **Because the foolishness of God is wiser than men; and the weakness of God is stronger than men.**"

The people that do not want to go out and preach the Gospel (evangelize), think that they can sit on their comfortable chairs at home and just 'bind' people to God's will and the people will be saved. It is a lack of willingness to inconvenience themselves in going out to evangelize. **Therefore, 'binding people to God's will' is a lazy man's approach to preaching the Gospel and God hates it.**

Chapter 9
New Age Movement and Other Witchcraft Organizations

The Composition of the New Age Doctrine

The New Age movement includes elements of older spiritual and religious traditions ranging from **atheism** (no God) and **monotheism** (one God) through **pantheism** (nature being identical with God), **pandeism** (creator becoming the universe) and **panentheism** (God in everything and everything in God) to **polytheism** (many gods). Their doctrines are a combination of **science, psychology, astronomy, cology** and **Gaia philosophy** or the **Gaia hypothesis** (worship of the earth as god — 'mother earth').

Also, New Age practices and philosophies sometimes draw inspiration from major world religions such as **buddhism, taoism, Christianity, hinduism, Judaism, islam, satanism, sikhism** and **chinese folk religion.** As a result, New Age is a combination of anything and everything. They infused the different doctrines from different religions with an **earth-centered worship, self-help, motivational psychology, holistic health, parapsychology, meta-physical consciousness practice** and **quantum physics.** As you can clearly see, they have a pluralistic and an all-inclusive approach to their dogmas but **the essence of what they produced** (New Age) is demonic. **Meaning that after mixing all the different selected doctrines of different religions with science and occultic beliefs, they developed the so-called New Age which is nothing but a demonic movement spear headed by atheists.**

Satanic Influence in the New Age Doctrine

Satanism is at the root of the New Age doctrines. Their doctrines are in line with Aleister Crowley or the *Crowleyan Satanism.* **Crowley was not only a confessed Satanist but**

was also the father of the Hippie movement from which popular New Age teachings first became entrenched in Western countries. He did not hide the fact that he was a satanist when he began and as such, you see a lot of satanic practices tied up in the New Age worship and beliefs. They worship the earth, the sun and anything else that they can worship because Crowley believed in the worship of everything except the **One True God** that created him. The New Age movement involves:

- Satanic doctrines
- Demonic meditation/eastern meditation
- Metaphysical practices (trying to evolve into gods or some other entity rather than remain human)
- Earth worship or new earth consciousness
- Chanting
- Falling into trances
- Use of hallucinogens such as opium or marijuana

New Age meditations are often influenced by eastern philosophy, mysticism, yoga, hinduism and buddhism. Also, hypnosis, tarot cards, ouija boards, psychic readings, crystal balls, palm readings, astral projection, and horoscopes. They all **should be considered total witchcraft practices because they all derive their power from satan and not from the God of the Bible.** If you have ever practiced any of these, you need to repent and ask God for forgiveness. He will forgive you, deliver you and shut the door to these evil spirits in your life. He will also remove the negative consequences resulting from your involvement in New Age practices.

The Hippie Influence and New Age

The New Age Movement gained momentum in the 1960s because of the rebellious hippie trends and their desire to fuse self-help psychology, metaphysical doctrines and other various Indian gurus' practices into their lifestyle. They helped to advance the evil movement and exposed many of the next generations to the demons that they were fraternizing with.

Their lifestyle and their New Age doctrines were very twisted with no sexual restrains. **They not only left the door wide open to evil doctrines but brought all forms of drug abuse and moral laxity home with them.** They called it a 'sexual revolution' but the devil saw it as a doorway to pervert a nation. Society is still suffering from the effects of the hippie and New Age Movements.

Many of the youths or young adults today have a serious battle with the spirits of drug abuse and sexual perversion as a direct outcome of the hippie and New Age movements. As a result, if you are dealing with someone who has been involved in the New Age or who has its doctrine in his or her bloodline, the person has to renounce the covenants made on his or her behalf with the spirits of New Age. Those who practiced New Age or read New Age books also need to repent.

A Word about Yoga

I know that some Christians consider yoga to be innocent and good. Those who say this are ignorant of the root of yoga. It is a form of worship in the religions from which it originates — hinduism, buddhism, jainism, etc. Those who practice hinduism believe that their **deity called shiva** gave them the practice of yoga as a form of worship. Many Christians attend yoga classes as a form of exercise and they do not see anything wrong with it but before you get involved in yoga, it pays to check out its roots. **My question is:** Is this yoga practice from a hindu 'god' something that a Christian should get involved in? Should we fraternize with this spirit?

I know that many believers have tried to 'christianize' yoga in their attempt to justify their involvement in it. **There are those who are promoting yoga practice to Christians and telling church leaders to host yoga classes as a form of whipping their congregations into shape.** As a result, you now have what I call 'yoga prophets' who are actively holding yoga classes in some churches. They forgot what the

Lord said in **Matthew 7:17-18** that <u>a corrupt tree cannot bring forth good fruit</u>:

> "Even so every good tree bringeth forth good fruit; **but a corrupt tree bringeth forth evil fruit.** *18* **A good tree cannot bring forth evil fruit, <u>neither can a corrupt tree bring forth good fruit</u>.**"

What good thing can a Christian receive from **shiva** or how can you change the tree that **shiva** planted?

How the Lord Saved Me from the Yoga Spirit

Always remember what the Lord said in the scripture above because it will keep you from being dragged into the things of darkness. Below is how He saved me from getting involved in yoga.

Some years ago, the instructors in the place where I was exercising decided that they were going to start yoga classes. One of the instructors who was going to teach the classes told us about it excitedly. I told them that I was a Christian and that I did not think that I should get involved in yoga. They responded that they too were Christian and went on to say how it was all purely exercise that had nothing to do with demons or religion. This conversation took place on a Friday and they told me that the classes will start the following Monday.

I did not think much about the conversation afterwards but I was shocked when on Sunday morning (the day before the classes began) the Lord showed me a vision of the hindu and buddhist spirits entering the building that was going to be used for the yoga classes. **According to the Lord's explanation to me, they have a right to be there because yoga in all its form is in their honor and worship!**

Chapter 10
Religions with Satanic and Witchcraft Roots

Witchcraft Roots of Pagan Religions

One of the reasons that we need to know about the witchcraft roots of pagan religions is their **covenant influence** on the bloodline of Christians. **Our God is a God of covenant and as a result, He honors every covenant that we make; even when the covenant is with the devil.** As I showed you before, the covenant that Adam made with the devil is still valid today in the life of everyone that is not yet 'born again'! As a 'born again' Christian, you need to renounce the covenant that your relatives or the generation before you made with the devil through pagan religious practices. We cannot mixed the old (pagan religion) with Christianity as stated in **Matthew 9:16-17:**

> **"No man putteth a piece of new cloth unto an old garment, for that which is put in to fill it up taketh from the garment, and the rent is made worse.** *17* Neither do men put new wine into old bottles: else the bottles break, and the wine runneth out, and the bottles perish: **but they put new wine into new bottles, and both are preserved."**

One of the reasons that I am writing about this topic is to alert Christians to the roots and witchcraft connection that form the core of the generational curses that they are battling with today. As people now freely move from one country to another to live temporarily or permanently, many of them are taking their pagan religious practices with them to their new countries. As a result, many countries have recently become opened to the 'new demons' that the newcomers brought with them. Today, you cannot hope to find the witchcraft spirit only in Africa, the Caribbean, Asia, Cuba, Puerto Rico, Middle East, New Zealand alone because there are now santeria worship houses, hindu temples, buddhist temples,

Asian religious temples and Muslim mosques and African religious houses in many nations in the Western world.

Pagan Religions of Europe

Even in the face of Christianity, the medieval pagan religions of European countries such as the Druids and Celtic, the Angles, and other Germanic tribes still have great influence in the lives of the people in these regions. As a result, they are fast turning away from Christianity because of the 'open doors' that the pagan religious beliefs and practices of the ancient people represent in Europe today. **The Europeans' pagan beliefs and practices form the core of the witchcraft activities that you see in Western countries today.**

This form of witchcraft is hardest to discern because it is woven into the Western culture and mindset. **As a result, earth based doctrines of the 'The Big Bang theory' and the 'Evolutionary Theory' which claim that matter (the universe) just sprang out of chaos and that it has been involving ever since, are embraced without questions. They basically reject the notion that God exists and that He created the universe.** Due to this very liberal mindset, they use science to explain away the things of God as being nothing but superstitious beliefs. This is a very serious form of witchcraft that is currently affecting a lot of people through scientific and philosophical beliefs. **It took control of the Western mind and turned it against God.**

This liberal mindset has also resulted in placing personal freedoms above the Word of God. As a result, you now have the 'new civil rights' claim in Western countries that everyone basically has the right or freedom to practice even the things that God said are sins. These pagan or hedonistic practices along with open rebellion against God and demonic tattoos or emblem are now widely accepted in Western countries. We will do well to remember the Prophet Samuel's words in **1 Samuel 15:23:**

"For <u>rebellion</u> is as the <u>sin of witchcraft</u>, and <u>stubbornness</u> is as <u>iniquity</u> and <u>idolatry</u>. **Because thou hast rejected the word of the LORD, he hath also rejected thee** ..."

Today, Christians of European descent or <u>Christians with Western education have to fight knowingly or unknowingly to overcome these pagan influences in their subconscious minds. The reason is because these beliefs seek to rob them of their faith as the scientific studies make them walk by sight instead of faith</u>. **Truly, if left unchecked, the Western mind challenges what is written in the Bible by what scientists come up with in the labs.** They promote an atheistic lifestyle with their findings and as such, we have people walking away from the Bible and its teaching because they have now become well educated. If left alone, Western education breeds apostasy in the church. As a result of earning a PhD and a Master's degree at modern universities, some people begin to view the Bible as a superstitious or a primitive book that time, science and civilization has transcended. **As I said earlier, this type of witchcraft is very hard to discern because it is clothed in 'modernity'.** In other words, it is valued and highly esteemed because it is 'knowledge' and it is the 'current trend'.

Impact of the Pagan Religions of Egypt

The Egyptian Worship of Osiris, Isis and Horus has a worldwide impact; especially through Freemasonry and other occultic organizations. Atum, Ra and Horus are worshipped as the sun-gods and they are the deities that are worshipped in the **Temple of the sun-god of Egypt.** According to Egyptian mythology, **Osiris** was the king with a wife called **Isis** and a brother named **Set.** Both **Osiris** and **Isis** had a son called **Horus.** They represent some of the most important deities in Egyptian pagan religions, worship and witchcraft practices. The fact that the existence of these deities began from a pagan mythology immediately tells us that whatever practices and worships are derived from them cannot be godly because God Almighty deals in TRUTH. Although they are borne out of lies, the mythology of **Osiris, Isis, Horus** and **Set** is a vital aspect of the Egyptian religious codes of conduct and afterlife expectations. **They viewed the conflicts between these deities as battles between good and evil; with good prevailing over evil but bear in mind that this is all pagan and rooted in witchcraft.**

According to the mythological belief, **Set** was jealous of his older brother, **King Osiris** so he plotted to have him killed so that he can become king. **Set** made a casket designed to only fit his older brother, **King Osiris** and he threw a celebration party meant to trap his brother. At the party, he came up with a game which involved having each guest lay in the casket to see who would be the 'perfect fit' for the casket. Each guest took their turn to lie in the casket and nobody was the 'perfect fit' because the casket had been tailor made to fit only **King Osiris**. When **King Osiris'** turn came to lie in the casket, **Set** promptly closed and locked the casket. Thus, King Osiris died in the casket and he threw the casket into the Nile River.

Osiris's wife **Isis** went in search of the casket and found it and brought it home but **Set** cut the corpse of **King Osiris** into pieces and scattered it all over Egypt. **Again, Isis went in search of all the body parts and she found all of Osiris' body parts except for the male organ.** Through the spell that she **(Isis)** learned from her father, she recreated **Osiris'** male organ and she briefly brought **Osiris** back to life. **It is claimed that the same spell also gave Isis time to become pregnant by Osiris before he again died and she gave birth to Horus.** Since **Horus** was born after **Osiris'** resurrection, he became known as **a representation of new beginnings** and the **vanquisher** of the evil **Set** when he regained the throne from **Set**.

As you can see, there is the use of magic and spells in Egyptian mythology and this particular mythology is the core of most Egyptian religious life. **When you read or hear** about the Egyptian mythology, you might think that it has nothing to do with you or modern society but it is amazing how their beliefs have infiltrated churches that believe in the Lord Jesus Christ through the Roman Catholic Church; even in their order of worship! Some of the churches that broke away from the Catholic Church kept the order of worship. The Catholic Church is filled with paganism from Egypt and Rome.

Egyptian Impact on the Roman Catholic Church

In recent years, there has been a movement even within the Spirit-filled churches to become bishops. **In becoming bishops, pastors that previously have no connection with the Roman Catholic Church and its yoke of bondage are now willingly putting their necks in the yoke of the Vatican.** This is because there is a <u>false claim</u> that 'to be a bona fide bishop, your bishophood has to be traced all the way to Saint Peter in the Roman Catholic Church and Vatican!'

As a result, those who become 'genuine bishops' are ordained by another bishop who was ordained by a Roman Catholic Cardinal that was himself ordained by the Pope! Just with this desire to become bishops, even Spirit-filled pastors are now placing themselves under the Pope and under the Roman Catholic Church. **The danger is that when you become a member of one of these types of churches or denominations with a leader that is a bishop, you come into an active covenant with the Egyptian spirits from the courts of Isis and Horus <u>without knowing it.</u>**

In essence, I will say that today, the worship of **Osiris**, **Isis** and **Horus** has found its way into the lives of many Christians through **Rome** and the **Roman Catholic Church**, the **Freemasonry** and other **mystic practices**. I experienced how an innocent Christian can get afflicted in a church as a result of the pagan practices within the church seven months after I got saved. **I ended up in a psychiatric hospital because**

of what happened to me in the Roman Catholic Church 'Mass' (church service) that I had attended. I innocently and ignorantly kissed the Roman Catholic **Monstrance** without knowing that it was straight out of the Temple of **Isis**:

A Picture of the Monstrance

My Affliction Inside the Roman Catholic Church

After my salvation, I started going to 'Mass' several times a week because I became extra religious and they last about 30 minutes. One Friday, I went to the 'Benediction of the Holy Sacrament' *(worshipping the communion bread)* and what happened in the service was bizarre and frightening at the time. Simply put, all hell broke loose against me by the end of the 'Mass'. The part of the account is narrated in my book titled, ***Unveiling the God-mother***, pages 88-89:

"At the end of the service, the priest placed the Eucharist in the center of a golden stand with a long-stemmed handle and a round top with sunrays--the sunburst (pictured above). ***The Roman Catholic Church calls it the 'monstrance', but what I did not know was that in reality, it was the Egyptian symbol of the sun-god!*** *I was ignorant of the meaning of the symbol and the significance of this particular religious rite that took place at the end of the service. All I knew was that at the end of the service, almost everyone in the sanctuary walked up to the Priest and kissed the Monstrance that had the Eucharist in its center.*

The Priest had raised it up for the people to come and kiss before leaving the sanctuary. I clearly heard the Holy Spirit's instruction, 'do not join them' as I stood in line. Again, in disobedience to the Holy Spirit, I thought to myself, the Eucharist is the body of Christ; why can't I go up and kiss it? My belief at the time was that the devil couldn't tamper with the Eucharist. So ignoring the Holy Spirit's words, I felt it was safe to go up and kiss the Monstrance as a reverence of Jesus. So, I went up to the Priest and kissed it. **What I did not know at the time was that I had just kissed the sun-god symbol of Nimrod and Semiramis and that I had unleashed hordes of demons against me!** *What happened after I kissed that monstrance God used to change my life forever.*

As I turned to walk away after kissing it, I began to see people as ghosts! I could see the spirits (good and bad) inside people as in an X-ray. Almost every one of the evil spirits in the people I met, tried to scare me like Dracula does in horror movies by suddenly leaping at me. Although they were trying to terrify me, I tried to be brave and not to show any sign of weakness. I left the sanctuary, and I decided to go into some of the shops in the mall to clear my eyes and my head by window-shopping. Three days later, I was in the psychiatric hospital..."

The worship of the sun-god dates back to Nimrod and his wife Semiramis in Babel! The worship of **Isis** and **Horus** is just a version of it. Sun-god worship is still widely practiced by many pagan religions of today and it includes the modern goddess movement and interfaith organizations such as the Fellowship of **Isis**. What was unknown to me at the time was that the worship of **Osiris, Isis** and **Horus** had made its way into the denominational churches through Rome and especially through the Roman Catholic Church. I also did not know that the whole 'search for enlightenment' in Freemasonry is based on **Isis'** search for the male organ of **Osiris** her husband! The worship of **Osiris, Isis, Horus** (Egyptian gods) form the basis of the Freemasonry and other Western occultic organizations that some people and their previous generations in this country were members of. By their memberships in these occultic organizations that have Egyptian roots, their ancestors or past generations helped to introduce the witchcraft practices and beliefs from Egypt into their family bloodline.

The Obelisk as Osiris' Missing Male Organ

The Secret societies and occultic groups whose practices involve the 'quest for enlightenment', adopt the **Obelisk** (the symbol of Osiris' missing male organ) as one of their prominent symbols. For example, the various 'degrees' in Freemasonry that the members graduate through are in fact, the steps in the 'search for enlightenment' and they are nothing but the steps of **Isis** in her quest for Osiris' missing male organ. This is the final enlightenment that a mason discovers at the highest levels of his quest. It is why they adopted the **obelisk** as their symbol of enlightenment. The **Freemasonry's obelisk** in Washington D.C called the '**Washington Monument**' is nothing but **Isis' symbol of Osiris' missing male organ**! You also have other Freemasonry objects or buildings like **the Pentagon** and **National sites** and the general layout of the city of Washington, DC that trace their roots all the way back to Egypt.

The Freemason's influence is even in the money such as the $1 bill that prominently displays the Egyptian pyramid as well as the 'eye of Horus' for all to see. The Freemasons did not hide the desire to put their marks on this nation and they did. As a result, when you are fighting Freemasonry in your family and you only pray it away back to your grandfather, you will not be successful because you are not dealing with its roots which is all the way back to Washington, DC and Egypt. This is why many wonder why their prayers against Freemasonry are not removing its negative effects from their lives. They do not know that they are leaving its Egyptian roots intact when they pray and as a result, the strongman behind Freemasonry does not obey them. **Freemasonry is a satanic organization because at the head of it is pure worship of satan.**

Those who practice Freemasonry might not have the ability to fly or engage in astral projection (going out of their bodies) like other satanic mystic organizations such as the Rosicrucians and Ekists of Eckankar, but it is still a form of witchcraft. It leaves a door in a person's life for satan and his demons to come and go as they please. You must renounce it from your life.

The Impact of Roman Religion

Also, certain Roman pagan beliefs have found their way into the main stream activities of the world today and many Christians also get afflicted as a result. The ancient Roman religion involved the **Vestals or the Vestal Virgins.** They were priestesses of **Vesta; the virgin goddess** of the **hearth** (fireplace), **home**, and **family**. The Romans believed that the laws of their ancestors provided for the **Vestal virgins** and the **Priests** of the 'gods' to foretell future events and as a reward, they are to live a life of a moderate maintenance and privileges. **The Vestals where virgins that were in the temple of the goddess Vesta.** The Vestals were freed from the usual social obligations to marry and bear children so they took vows of chastity in order to devote themselves to the study and the correct observance of state rituals.

There were also **Priests** (males) but some of the rituals of the **Vestals** were not required of the male **Priests**. In General, **Vestal virgins** and **Priests** were young men and young ladies. **The Vestals and Priests were committed to the Nunnery and Priesthood at a young age (taken before puberty) and were sworn to celibacy for a period of 30 years**. The **Vestals** had much power ascribed to them because they were the 'goddesses' or the 'oracles' that spoke for the 'gods' that the Romans worshiped. **History has it that if a person was on the way to be executed and a Vestal virgin happened to be passing by, they have to let the person go. Rome cannot execute the person because the person saw the Vestal virgin.**

We are still dealing with the remnant of Vestal practice today in the form of the **Roman Catholic Nuns and Priests**! When Rome fell, the Bishop that was over Rome (the **Bishop of Rome** as he was previously called) became the leader of the Church, in place of the Emperor. **He immediately annexed the power of the Roman Emperors and adopted the practice of Emperor Worship under the title of Pope!** As Pope, the former **Bishop of Rome** never really reformed the Emperors' practices were that were not in line with the Gospel of Jesus Christ but used them to enlarge his position.

As a result, you still see the pagan practices of Rome within the Roman Catholic Church today; just like the **Vestal Virgins**, you have **Priests** and **Nuns that are celibate.** Instead of worship services like other churches, you have the Roman pagan practice **'saying of the Mass'** and they carry the Pope around in a **Pope Mobile** just as they carried the Emperors around in ancient Rome. **You have to understand where your roots have been; especially if you have been in the Roman Catholic Church so that you can repent of Roman pagan practices.**

The Impact of Greek Idolatry and Mythology

Greek mythology embodies the **myths** and **teachings** of **ancient Greeks** that tell of their 'gods', their origin, heroes, nature, the importance of their ritual practices and cults. Mythology was a part of the pagan religion of ancient Greece and prominent among them is their belief in many 'gods' of which the most prominent are; **Titans**, **Zeus**, **Olympians**, **Pan** and **Dionysus. In this book, I <u>will focus</u> on the ones that influence things like the <u>Olympic Games</u> and the <u>people of European descent</u> today.**

Zeus and Europa's Influence on Europe and the World

According to Greek mythology, **Zeus** (the Greek god) turned himself into a white bull and carried away a Phoenician (modern day Lebanon) maiden called **Europa** who was from a prominent family and lineage. Zeus raped her and she produced children. The European continent is named after her and her descendants are called Europeans. The Greek statue of Europa shows her sitting on a white bull that represents Zeus.

Greek Depiction of Europa on a White Bull

Since 1958, those who claim Europa as their common ancestor have organized themselves into what is known as the **European Union** or EU of today! This is why the **symbol of the European Union** or EU in Brussels, Belgium is **Europa sitting on a bull. All they did was modernize Europa and the bull with a contemporary artwork showing the pagan roots of the union for all to see.**

Depiction of Europa on a Bull at EU Headquarters in Brussels

Therefore, to call yourself a European is to claim this demonic lineage which traces your ancestry to a pagan mythology from ancient Greece. Can you imagine being the descendant of a bull and a human? It is absurd and paganistic. It does matter where you claim to be from before you became a 'born again' Christian because after your new birth, you cannot subscribe to this type of paganism. You have to renounce her as your ancestor because failure to do so will unleash the spirits behind this false doctrine to declare warfare against you for jumping camp. This is one of the reasons why Europe is increasingly becoming apostate and pagan; it is becoming a dark continent spiritually because the leaders chose to forsake God and revert to idolatry. Revelation 17:3-4 talks about a woman sitting on a scarlet beast (the attire of a harlot) and she is none other than Europa!

The Greek Pythia's Influences on the World

The Greek Pythia is also known as the **Oracle of Delphi.** She was the **Priestess of the Temple of Apollo at Delphi** which was located on the slopes of Mount Parnassus. **This Priestess was widely credited for her prophecies** that were **believed to have been inspired by Apollo; the son of Zeus.** The name **Pythia** is from the Greek verb **Pythein which means** '*to rot*' in reference to the decomposition of the body of the **monstrous serpent Python** after <u>she</u> was **slain** by **Apollo** and her body was left to rot.

One common view has been that the **Priestess** or the **Pythia** delivered oracles in a 'frenzied state' induced by vapors rising from a chasm (cleft) in the rock and that she spoke **'gibberish'** which older and well-seasoned priests reshaped into mysterious prophecies that are preserved even today in the Greek literature. **What this shows us is that the Pythia or Oracle at Delphi is a form of witchcraft practice.** I will shortly discuss how it still influences countries through the **Olympic Games** today but first, let us look at its demonic origin.

Origin of the Pythia or the Oracle at Delphi

There are many stories about the origin of the **Oracle at Delphi**. According to **Diodorus Siculus,** a 1st century BC writer, a goat herder named **Coretas** noticed one day that one of his goats who fell into a <u>chasm</u> (a deep, steep-sided opening in the earth's surface; an abyss or gorge) and the goat began to behave strangely. **Upon entering the <u>chasm,</u> the goat herder became <u>filled with a divine presence from the rock</u> and as a result, he could <u>see outside of the present into the past and the future.</u>** He excitedly shared his experience with nearby villagers and it generated mass interest among them. **Many people began to visit the <u>chasm</u> in order to experience the convulsions and inspirational trances and some of the people were believed to have disappear into the cleft of the <u>chasm</u> in their frenzied state.**

By 1600 BC, **a shrine was erected** at the <u>chasm</u> and people began worshiping there. The villagers chose **a single young woman** (unmarried) as the medium for the divine inspirations from the 'gods'. She spoke on behalf of the 'gods' and was known as the **Pythia** or **Oracle at Delphi. She was the mouth-piece of the 'gods' at Delphi and she lived in the Temple. She received 'words' as 'oracles' and she spoke them as 'prophecies' to the older priests.** The **Pythia** (Priestess) inspired the Roman's **Vestals Virgins** that were the **predecessor** of the **Roman Catholic Nuns.**

The Pythian Games as the Origin of the Olympic Games

The Pythian games are the forerunner to the **Olympic Games** of today and they were held <u>every four years</u> in honor of **Apollo** at the **sanctuary in Delphi** because **Apollo** was regarded as <u>the 'god' of sports, physical fitness, light and sun</u> *(source: Wikipedia).* In the inner part of the temple was an **hearth** (a fireplace) where the 'eternal flame' supposedly 'burns'. The **Olympic Games** of today began at this pagan site; at the Oracle of Delphi and the Torch of the Olympic

Games today is a pagan 'eternal flame'! **At the start of the games, they perform a worship ceremony of Apollo before going up to Mount Olympus to conduct the games; still in honor of the Apollo, their 'god'.** When the **Roman Empire** came along, it simply elaborated on the games and built huge theaters and coliseums for them. It helped to transport or transfer the **Olympics Games** that were meant to worship Apollo in Greece to the Western world.

As a Christian, you wonder how rational and intelligent people can set aside the Bible which is clearly the Word of God and choose to believe Greek mythology and the craziness that they tell. For instance, how can a piece of rock that cracked suddenly possess some power as a 'god' to talk to a person? Even after the myth stated that the messages from the so-called 'gods' were 'gibberish', people were still willing to receive them as divine messages.

The World Impact of the Pythia and Olympic Games

Today, the whole world comes together every four years under the umbrella of the **Olympic Games** with a **Torch** that sometimes comes straight out of the **Temple of Apollo in Delphi**, Greece. Just as in the ancient worship of Apollo, a **Delphi Priestess** is accompanied by some other women *(modern type of vestal virgins)* to perform the Greek pagan ceremony before lighting the Torch. **She then gives it to a bearer and it is carried through different nations before it arrives at the nation that is hosting the Olympic Games that year!** This is the modern witchcraft that is being celebrated by the so-called 'civilized nations'. **They do this because they became 'civilized' the Greek mythological way!**

The Impact of the Greek Mindset on the World through Education

The pagan religious practices that directly influence most societies in Western countries today; even the school system, the court system and governments are based on the

Greek system of thinking. **In other words, Greek pagan beliefs have greatly influenced Western educational systems and institutions of higher learning in many countries today.** As a result, children going to school get fed these mythological beliefs and they are told to challenge the Bible. The problem is that they are pagan religions that operate by witchcraft and divinations. They also promote a false sense of wisdom which the Bible calls the **'wisdom of this world'** and as we saw earlier, those who are influenced by the 'Greek mindset' view the belief in the Word of God as foolishness — **1 Corinthians 1:18-25:**

> **"For the preaching of the cross is to them that perish foolishness; but unto us which are saved it is the power of God.** *19* For it is written, I will destroy the wisdom of the wise, and will bring to nothing the understanding of the prudent. *20* Where is the wise? where is the scribe? where is the disputer of this world? <u>hath not God made foolish the wisdom of this world</u>? *21* For after that in the wisdom of God the world by wisdom knew not God, it pleased God by the foolishness of preaching to save them that believe.
>
> *22* **For the Jews require a sign, and the <u>Greeks seek after wisdom</u>:** *23* But we preach Christ crucified, unto the Jews a stumblingblock, **and unto the Greeks foolishness;** *24* But unto them which are called, both Jews and Greeks, Christ the power of God, and the wisdom of God. *25* **Because the foolishness of God is wiser than men; and the weakness of God is stronger than men."**

You do not want to make a covenant with the spirits behind the Greek mythology because they will contend with your Christian walk as you try to exercise your faith. They do this in the mind of those who are under their influence by creating a 'double mindedness' or unbelief in them and as a result, the people begin to view the Word of God as

foolishness or to challenge what it says. To prove the point of the scripture above, all we need to do is take a look at some very well educated people and we can clearly see the devastating effects of the Greek promotion of the 'wisdom of this world'. **As you try to preach the Gospel, you will come across many of them that think that they are too educated to believe what is written in the Bible. The end result is that these people become atheists.**

I have personally encountered people who view faith in the Word of God as foolishness because they are just too well educated to condescend to such belief. I also saw the world influence of the Greek mythology during the Olympic Games in Atlanta. I could not watch the opening and closing ceremonies because they both honored the sun-god of Egypt and Greece. Also, at the closing ceremony, they chose to play John Lennon's song, *Imagine* with the lyrics that tells the hearer to *imagine that there is: no heaven, no God, no religion, etc.*

John Lennon's goal was to spread atheism through self-worship but his life was cut short. There are those who share his goal and the organizers of the Olympic Games in Atlanta chose the Lennon goal as their message to the world. We need to be aware of when this type of active covenant with the Greek evil mythological belief is being made on our behalf so that we can say **no** to it. A lot of the generational curses that we are up against are the results of pagan religions and their witchcraft roots in our bloodline but sometimes, **cities** and **nations** also ignorantly invite these spirits against their citizens.

Pagan Religions Outlined in the Bible

The Bible tells us of **Tamuz** (the Assyrian and Babylonian god); **Molech** (the god of the Phoenicians and Canaanites); **Asthoreth** (the Zidonian god), **Chemosh** (the god of the Moabites) and **Dagon** (the pagan god of the Philistines) that helped to further establish religious activities that have their roots in witchcraft that still affect people today —**Judges 10:6:**

"And the children of Israel did evil again in the sight of the LORD, and served **Baalim**, and **Ashtaroth**, and the gods of Syria, and the **gods of Zidon**, and the **gods of Moab**, and the **gods of the children of Ammon**, and the **gods of the Philistines**, and forsook the LORD, and served not him."

For example, the name **Assyrian** is a Latin word derived from the name **Ashur**; the Assyrian 'god'. Other religious practices of the world that are outside of the worship of the Judeo-Christian God also fall into this category as well. God hates all idolatry and we that are His children should do our part to stay away from them. We should renounce all the covenants that the past generations made on our behalf with the spirits of idolatry. The information below will help you to know how to pray if you are a Christian from this part of the world.

The Countries Listed Above Are Now Known As Follows:

- **Assyria:** The remnant of the Assyrian people who are now almost exclusively Eastern Rite Assyrian Christians are an ethnic and religious minority in **northern Iraq, northeastern Syria, eastern Turkey** and **northwestern Iran**.

- **Philistine:** It consists of modern day city-states of **Gaza, Ashkelon, Ashdod, Ekron** and **Gath**.

- **Moab:** It is the historical name for a mountainous strip of land in **Jordan.**

- **Zidon:** Today, it is the third largest city in **Lebanon**.

- **Babylon:** Babylon is the region we now refer to as modern day **Iraq, Kuwait**, parts of **Syria**, Turkey and **Iran**.

- **Canaan:** It is the region that we now refer to as **the Levant**. It consists of **Lebanon, Israel, Palestine, western Jordon**, and **southwestern Syria**.

- **Phoenicia:** Is modern day **Lebanon**.

The pagan religious beliefs of these ancient people groups have evolved and are incorporated into some modern social beliefs, secret societies, and newer religious practices. If left in place by a new Christian, they can subject him or her to constant harassment by the spirits of poverty, ill health, vagabond lifestyle and many other afflictions. **The devil knows that he cannot kill Christians without working hard to get their cooperation so he tries to make their lives miserable.**

The KKK Organization
The ritual activities of the KKK organization makes it qualify as a witchcraft organization. It is highly demonic and involves:

- Nocturnal (nighttime) activities
- Hatred
- Satanic codes and oaths
- Satanic initiation ceremonies
- Use of blood
- Use of strange fire —cross burning
- Killings; hanging with a noose (human sacrifice)
- Dehumanization of certain races
- Demonic pride and an evil sense of racial superiority

Chapter 11
Characteristics of the Different Types of Witchcraft

Jesus Is the Light of the World

According to the Bible, **we were all born in sin** because **Adam's sin** (rebellion against God) was passed on to all mankind. Adam <u>knowingly</u> and <u>willfully disobeyed God's instruction</u> concerning the fruit from the **Tree of Knowledge of Good and Evil** and this **rebellious nature** (original sin) was inherited by every human being! What this means is that Adam plunged us all into darkness to be used by the devil at his pleasure to do all types of wickedness. **It also means that we became vulnerable to the devil to be used as pawns against God.**

Even man's attempts to gravitate towards God became perverted by the devil into all forms of demonic worship (satanic worship) in every society until God made a covenant with Abraham. Part of the terms of this covenant was the blessing of salvation through **Abraham's seed. God further told Abraham that the seed shall come through his legitimate son Isaac because God honors the legitimate family unit that He established through Adam and Eve** — Genesis 21:12:

> "And God said unto Abraham, Let it not be grievous in thy sight because of the lad *(Ishmael)*, and because of thy bondwoman *(Hagar, a slave)*; in all that Sarah hath said unto thee, hearken unto her voice; **for in Isaac shall thy seed be called.**"

This **seed** was revealed and manifested in the person of **Jesus Christ** as we see in **Galatians 3:16:**

> "**Now to Abraham and his** <u>seed</u> **were the promises made.** He saith not, <u>And to seeds, as of many</u>; but <u>as of one</u>, **And to thy seed,** <u>which is Christ</u>."

In other words, God in His love, made a way through Abraham's seed (**Jesus Christ**) to bring us all (humanity) out of darkness (satan's clutches) into His marvelous light. This is why the Lord Jesus said in **John 14:6:**

> "Jesus saith unto him, I am the way, the truth, and the life: **no man cometh unto the Father, but by me.**"

And also in **John 8:12:**

> "…**I am the** <u>light of the world</u>**: he that followeth me shall not walk in darkness,** but <u>shall have the light of life</u>."

As a result of this important work that God did for us in Christ to bring us out of darkness, anyone that rejects the Gospel of Jesus Christ, rejects the light that God sent to all humanity and the person remains in darkness or in the devil's clutches. This person also rejects the only way that God provided for us to get to Him; Jesus is <u>truly</u> the only way.

Children of Light & Children of Darkness

Besides being defined as lacking light, **darkness** is also defined as lacking enlightenment, lacking knowledge, evil in nature or effect and sinister. **In the Bible, darkness speaks of the devil and his works.** No matter how innocent or benign they may seem, the bottom line is that all acts of witchcrafts are acts of darkness from the devil. **They are what the Bible calls the works of darkness and those who are involved in them are called** <u>children of darkness</u>**.** We that are Christians are called the **children of light:**

> "Let no man deceive you with vain words: for because of these things cometh the wrath of God upon the <u>children of disobedience</u>. 7 Be not ye therefore partakers with them. 8 **For ye were sometimes darkness, but now are ye light in the Lord:** <u>walk as children of light</u>**:** 9 (For the fruit of the Spirit is in all

goodness and righteousness and truth;) *10* Proving what is acceptable unto the Lord. *11* **And have no fellowship with the unfruitful works of darkness, but rather reprove them.** *12* <u>For it is a shame even to speak of those things which are done of them in secret</u>. *13* **But all things that are reproved are made manifest by the light: for whatsoever doth make manifest is light"** (Ephesians 5:6-13).

And also in **1 Thessalonians 5:5:**

"Ye are all the **children of light**, and the children of the day: **we are not of the night, nor of darkness.**"

The Bible clearly tells us that those who accept the Lord Jesus as their Savior become the **children of light** and they **receive enlightenment from the Lord.** It is unfortunate that many people still join satanic organizations in their search for **enlightenment or self-discovery.** What they fail to realize is that only the Lord Jesus can bring a person out of darkness. **Those who insist on continuing their works of darkness show that they hate or reject the Gospel of Jesus Christ.** There is no middle ground between God and the devil. **You have only one choice: love one and hate the other.** Therefore, you cannot serve both God and the devil — **Matthew 6:24:**

"**No man can serve two masters:** <u>for either he will hate the one, and love the other; or else he will hold to the one, and despise the other</u>. Ye cannot serve God and <u>mammon</u> *(mammon or love of money is the devil's #1 tool for ensnaring souls)*."

There are those who have sold their souls out to the devil because of <u>the love of money</u> or just plain <u>insistence on rebellion against God</u>. They want nothing to do with the Lord Jesus and His Gospel of Salvation. This is why the Lord Jesus said that **those who are of the light** (of Him), gravitate towards the light and **those who are of darkness** (of the devil), gravitate towards darkness because their activities are evil — **John 3:19-21:**

> "<u>And this is the condemnation, that light is come into the world</u>, and **men loved darkness rather than light, because <u>their deeds were evil</u>.** *20* **<u>For every one that doeth evil hateth the light, neither cometh to the light, lest his deeds should be reproved.</u>** *21* **But he that <u>doeth truth cometh to the light</u>, that his deeds may be made manifest, that they are wrought in God."**

To demonstrate this point, a look at the buildings of the satanic churches, satanic covens, Freemasons and many other demonic organizations shows that there are <u>no windows</u>. **I am sure that a lot of people who pass by some of these buildings often wonder about them because it is unusual for a building or a house not to have windows that allow light in. The reason the buildings have no windows is because the activities that go on behind the closed doors are not of light.** They do not want light to come in because their works are done in darkness. They are in the depths of satan.

Members of witchcraft organizations are children of darkness; therefore, their activities are nocturnal. They swear dark oaths in secret and make evil vows in secret as they pledge their souls to the devil. Essentially, their covenants are nothing but **covenants with death.** They are the devil's children by their own free will.

Common Denominator in Secret Societies

Those who are into the more demonic secret societies like Freemason in the United States and other Western nations or the Freemason equivalent in Nigeria called Ogboni, have been known to storm the funeral preparations of their dead members to take the body part that the member pledged during initiation. In other words, **when they take over the** funeral arrangements, <u>they perform demonic rites in which they cut off the part of the body that the person pledged while the person was alive.</u> When they are finished with the dead body, they seal the casket and do not release it to the family as they follow it to its final place of burial!

Once sealed by them, the family members cannot even look into the casket because they do not want them to see the part of the person's body that they took. This happens all over the world in some of the more demonic secret societies. **The members not only give their souls to the devil but they also pledge their body parts at death.** It is a highly demonic characteristic.

Common Denominator among Witches

The witches that come to press people on their beds at night do not want to send charms or spells against the person. They just want to come into the person's room at night and get the job of killing the person done by themselves. Whereas the witches that are in satanic covens are more likely to send spells, curses and charms against people but make no mistake in the fact that they also want to kill you. **In other words, both the witches that fly at night and the ones in satanic covens <u>want you dead.</u>** The only difference is that they go about it in different ways. It is their common denominator.

Always remember that the witches in satanic covens are different from the more powerful types of witches in West Africa and elsewhere that have the ability to fly into their victims bedrooms at night. **An average West African will tell you that witches in satanic covens have amateur powers.** This is one of the reasons why when people from West Africa hear witches in satanic covens in the United States issue a threat such as, "You will see or I will show you," they laugh at them. They will even laugh at charms or spells from the witches in satanic covens because they know that the powers of the witches in satanic covens are limited compared to the more deadly demonic power by the flying witches and wizards.

You need this knowledge in order to effectively pray against each one of them when the occasion arises or before going to dislodge souls from them through evangelism. **You also need to remember that every 'born again' Christian can laugh at the powers of both the West African witches and the satanic coven witches because <u>we can overcome them all by the blood of Jesus.</u>** All you need to do is send their wickedness or their wicked devises back to them in the name of the Lord Jesus and to place the Cross and the blood of Jesus between you and them. **They cannot get to you when you do this because every satanic force bows at the name of the Lord Jesus!**

> **"That at the name of Jesus every knee should bow, of things in heaven, and things in earth, and things under the earth;** 11 And that every tongue should confess that Jesus Christ is Lord, to the glory of God the Father" (Philippians 2:10-11).

Common Denominator among Mediums

The common denominator among mediums is that they give messages or try to tell the future from satanic sources. **Soothsayers can give you messages and tell you fortunes while psychics do palm readings, tara cards reading and tea leaf readings.** There are items that people buy such as the ouija boards or even the fortune cookies in their attempts to find out what the future holds for them. **All of those things are forms of witchcraft because they are trying to get wisdom and knowledge from a source that is not God.** Remember this the next time you are given a fortune cookie (a message from the altar of Buddha) at a Chinese restaurant.

We are to live by the Word of God and we are to be led only by the Holy Spirit. Getting messages from another source that is not of God is being led by the devil. This is why we are told in **Romans 8:14** that:

"For as many as are **led by the Spirit of God**, they are the sons of God."

What this means is that if you are being led by another spirit such as the evil sources or even by a fortune cookie, you are outside of the Word of God. The Holy Spirit leads us by the Word of God and not by the word of Hare Krishna, Buddha, Mohammed, etc. Always remember what the Lord Jesus said in **Matthew 12:30** that:

"**He that is <u>not with me is against me</u>**; and he that gathereth not with me scattereth abroad."

That is why when you are not sure about a person that is speaking to you, the first thing you do is ask the Lord by what spirit the person talking to you. The Word of God is your immediate guide. Ask yourself if what the person is saying lines up with the Word of God. Below is my encounter with a lady 'performing cure' and how I tested her with the Word of God in order to see what powers she was using.

The Lady 'Performing Cure' with Demonic Powers

In *Chapter 3* of this book and under the subtitle, *The End Does Not Justify the Means,* I promised to discuss the African lady that was 'performing cure' with demonic powers. The reason I decided to include my encounter with this lady is because the Bible says in **1 John 4:1-3** that we should test every spirit to see if they are of God:

"**Beloved, believe not every spirit, but try the spirits whether they are of God: because many false prophets are gone out into the world.** 2 Hereby know ye the Spirit of God: Every spirit that confesseth that Jesus Christ is come in the flesh is of God: 3 **And every spirit that confesseth not that Jesus Christ is come in the flesh is not of God:** <u>and this is that spirit of antichrist</u>, whereof ye have heard that it should come; and even now already is it in the world."

*I remembered the above scripture during my encounter with the lady so I decided to test the spirit in the lady. I had never met her before but we went to visit her husband and he wanted us to meet his wife. We waited over 3 hours for her to come out of the room because her husband said that she was in the middle of something very important. When she finally emerged from the room, I knew that the person I went with was not going to say anything about how long we waited for her, so I told her that we have waited for her for over 3 hours. **She apologized and told us that she was performing a cure and it took that long to cure the person.***

*I was shocked by her statement because my first take on her was that she looked like she had gone mad; like someone who had just escaped from an asylum. Her hair was unkempt and her eyes were darting and piercing as if she was ready to leap at someone. Based on the fact that I did not see any evidence of the Spirit of God in her, I decided to test the spirit in her by asking her if she was 'born again' and if she was using the Bible in her cures. **She said to me, "I am beyond 'born again' and I have gone beyond the Bible!"** Right there in her answer, I knew that she was not using the power of the Holy Spirit so I said to her, "How do you perform these cures?"*

She said that she takes the person into the room and does her incantations to call forth whatever sickness or afflictions the person is suffering from into her own body. The person becomes free of the afflictions and she then goes into the woods to remove the ailments from her own body. That in essence is how she performs the 'cure' without any help from the Bible. She became furious when I told her that any power outside of the Bible is of the devil and therefore demonic. She countered my remarks by telling me that some churches have brought her to the United States several times to minister and that as a matter of fact, she had just returned from ministering at a church in Texas!

Can you image such a woman in some Spirit-filled churches laying hands on people and 'performing cure'? Undiscerning Christians will think that her laying hands on them is by the power of the Holy Spirit without knowing that she was using demonic powers. I was not surprised that she was not using the power of the Holy Spirit because most of the people with satanic affiliations will not confess Christ or seek His power. In summary, the common characteristics of the different types of witchcrafts are:

- They are anti-Christ.
- They do not worship the One True God in the Bible but worship satan.
- They are against righteousness and holiness as specified in the Bible.
- They use satanic powers.
- They engage in nocturnal activities.
- They use secrecy (secret oaths, vows and pledges and they all represent a 'covenant with death').
- They use evil sacrifices of animals and sometimes, humans.
- They use satanic agents such as witches, wizards or other intermediaries like the grandmasters or grand wizards).
- They use consultations or mediums with familiar spirits to divine, to enchant, to cast spells, to cast hexes, to send charms and incantations.
- They use soothsayers, graven images, amulets, idol worship, etc.
- They use sorcery through personal items such as clothing and hair.
- They use necromancy in 'communication with the dead' and the use of cemeteries.
- They send wickedness and evil assignments against people.

- They delight in acts of revenge and retaliation.
- They use graven images, amulets, talisman, etc.
- They use ungodly fire.
- They make people's souls to fly at night (not 'born again' Christians).
- They peep or spy on people's progress.
- They mutter or chew at people's ears at night.
- They are observers of times (seasons or full moon).

Chapter 12
Things that Invite the Witchcraft Spirit

Walking in Rebellion

The original sin (rebellion) that Adam committed against God opened the door for all the sins that you see in the world today to come in. **Disobedience** or **rebellion** against God's Word is the root of all sins and it the invention of the devil. The devil deceived Eve in the Garden to rebel against God and in turn, Eve seduced Adam to rebel against God. The sin brought death and chaos into God's perfect creation and turned Cain against God and against his brother Abel. As a result, the devil is very much aware of the effectiveness of the <u>use of rebellion in damning a human soul</u> and he uses it. **Those who choose to rebel against God's Word invite the devil and witchcraft is just one of the devil's tools.**

In His mercy, God made a way in His Son, Jesus Christ for all humanity to come out of rebellion against Him. **Unfortunately, many people are still choosing to reject the Word of God that comes to them through the Gospel and to remain in their rebellious state against God.** According to the Lord, those who do this leave themselves open to the devil to afflict them with anything that He wants including steering them into witchcraft activities. Also, the Bible tells us in **1 Samuel 15:23** that the sin of rebellion itself is comparable to the act of witchcraft:

> "For **rebellion is as the sin of witchcraft**, and stubbornness is as iniquity and idolatry. Because thou hast rejected the word of the LORD, he hath also rejected thee from being king."

Walking in Envy and Jealousy

Those who practice witchcraft use envy and jealousy as a reason to launch an assignment against a person. The witchcraft spirit is attracted to those who walk in envy and jealousy because they provide it with reasons to launch evil attacks. Therefore, by walking in envy and jealousy, you attract the witchcraft spirit and you make it your ally. The Lord once showed me a vision of someone in my family that I had never had any problem with in the physical realm as she was walking around in the spiritual realm looking for someone who will join her to launch an attack against me. I asked the Lord why the person was doing it because I have never had any quarrels with her and He said that it was because I was doing what the person had wanted to do but could not. Therefore, she became jealous of me.

Witches help those who have envy and jealousy against a person to launch an attack as they hear the person speak their envy or jealousy. Also, witches hate to see those that they know or that are close to them prosper. Their goal is usually to destroy a person's prosperity or kill those who are trying to prosper. Therefore, to keep witchcraft assignments away, we have to purpose not to walk in envy and jealousy ourselves. Have you ever had something that is really good about to happen to you and you speak in confidence to someone about it and the next thing you know, the thing never happens after that? As I stated before, this is usually the case when someone goes on a job interview and he or she is given an assurance that the job will be theirs. The person goes home and speaks to a relative or a friend and after that, they get a phone call that the job has been offered to someone else. The devil usually eavesdrops on a person's conversation through those who carry the witchcraft spirit in their bloodline and are filled jealousy. They report any prosperity shared with them to the devil's agents for destruction. Jealousy is evil.

Walking in Covetousness

Covetousness is rooted in the pride of, I am better than them: why them and not me? As a result of a person perceiving him or herself to be better suited for something or someone than another, the person begins to covet and to scheme on how to deprive the owner of that which they covet. The devil invented covetousness so he will immediately send his witchcraft spirit to help the person out. As a result, the person then becomes a thief, an adulterer, a murder, etc. Yes, there are people who covet what other people have to the point of taking the life of the owner.

The devils come to the aid of those who are covetous and they use witchcraft to destroy marriages and ruin the lives of innocent children by driving their victims (parents) with lustful desires in the nighttime until they commit the sin. As Christians, we know that we are not defined by the abundance of what we have but by the "Christ in us the hope of glory" (Colossians 1:27). This is why the Bible tells us in **Hebrews 13:5** to avoid covetousness and to be satisfied with what we have:

> "**Let your conversation be without covetousness**; and **be content with such things as ye have:** for he hath said, I will never leave thee, nor forsake thee."

Walking in Hatred and Resentment

Walking in hatred and resentment will make one a vessel that the witchcraft spirit uses as reason to launch an attack against a person. Hatred and resentment are also the devil inventions; they aid him in helping people carry out the works of the flesh of which witchcraft is one. Many people are not aware that although they go to church and read the Bible, they can still be the devil's tool to attack people as they walk in hatred and resentment towards the person.

We must not let the devil use us as his tools by making sure that we have no hatred or resentment towards others. **A good example of how hatred and resentment make a person the devil's tool to offer him human sacrifices and false worship is the KKK.** The members are driven by the witchcraft spirit to burn crosses (false worship) and hang those that they hate and resent (sacrifice). **Afterwards, they will go to church and participate in worship service without realizing that they also worship and offer human sacrifices to the devil by their KKK activities.** This is why their descendants must renounce this witchcraft spirit from their bloodline in order to be free of it and its negative consequences. Failure to do this brings the judgement of God that says, "… for whatsoever a man soweth, that shall he also reap" (Galatians 6:7). The family will keep reaping death and destruction until they repent.

Walking in Unforgiveness

Although you go to church every Sunday, when you walk in unforgiveness, you might be giving ammunition to the witchcraft spirit and unleashing its assignment against someone without knowing it. The poison that unforgiveness represents attracts the witchcraft spirit who then tries to help you destroy the person that you are refusing to forgive. This is why God hates unforgiveness because it is destructive and plays into the devil's hands.

We all need to realize that there is no middle ground when it comes to forgiveness and unforgiveness. **Forgiveness brings life and unforgiveness brings death.** God forgave us in His Son Jesus Christ and He wants us to forgive those who do us wrong because our problem is not with **flesh** and **blood** (man) but with the devil and his hosts of principalities, powers, rulers of darkness and spiritual wickedness. There are spirits that actually operate through people and try to make them hate others and refuse to forgive them of any wrong. They also want to plant the desire to harm others in these people. We must all run from unforgiveness in order to keep the devil away.

Seeking Revenge and Retaliation

Some people who refuse to forgive seek revenge and retaliation. God does not want us to avenge ourselves. Therefore, those who seek to avenge themselves by acts of retaliation, make themselves available for the devil because this is the goal of the witchcraft spirit. It will immediately come to the aid of anyone who wants to carry out any act of revenge or retaliation. Therefore, we must heed God's Word in **Romans 12:17-21:**

> "**Recompense to no man evil for evil.** Provide things honest in the sight of all men. *18* **If it be possible, as much as lieth in you, live peaceably with all men.** *19* Dearly beloved, <u>avenge not yourselves, but rather give place unto wrath</u>: for it is written, **Vengeance is mine; I will repay, saith the Lord.** *20* Therefore if thine enemy hunger, feed him; if he thirst, give him drink: for in so doing thou shalt heap coals of fire on his head. *21* **Be not overcome of evil, but overcome evil with good.**"

Walking in Offense and Anger

Throughout my life, I had occasions of making people angry and people making me angry without paying attention to how the spirit of anger and offense operate. Little did I know that if someone picks up an offense or anger against you, he or she can unleash a spiritual warfare against you with the help of the witchcraft spirit. The Lord wanted me to learn about the workings of these 'combo spirits' when the occasion arose one day.

I went to a local store to buy some items and one of the items was marked $2. When I got to the register, I set my basket down and the cashier (a foreign lady) began to ring them up. She got to the item that was marked $2 and she said, "Oh, no, this is $4." In response I said, "We are both looking at it marked $2; I just walked through the door and this is the price on it." I told her to go and check the rest of the same items and she will see that they were all marked $2.

She said that her manager had changed the price in the office but she forgot to put the new price on all of them. I then told her that I *was not going to let her talk me into paying $4 for something that was clearly marked $2. The lady got angry at me because I refused to pay the price that she was supposed to have marked the item. Her manager who happened to be within a few feet away came over. He told the lady to ring up the item at the sticker price. I told her that in America, people pay what the sticker price says; especially if the sticker price has not been tampered with but she was still furious. I went home without realizing the extent of her anger and the fact that she had witchcraft in her bloodline.*

That night, she came flying into my bedroom screaming war and I was like you are barking up the wrong tree. I unleashed the blood of Jesus and the Word of God against her. As I was rebuking her, the Lord spoke to me saying, "The lady told you that the price changed and that she forgot to put the new price sticker on the item. It was an honest mistake on her part but you did not listen." He then told me that He judges and makes war in righteousness and that if I want Him to always defend me, He needs to always see me on the side of righteousness in every situation. He said, "When I come on the scene, I want to first see you standing in righteousness. If you are on the side of righteousness, I will defend you even if it means annihilating an entire city of wicked people just for you; I will do it." He pointed me to **Revelation 19:11:**

"And I saw heaven opened, and behold a white horse; <u>and he that sat upon him was called Faithful and True,</u> and **in righteousness he doth judge and make war."**

I repented for insisting on paying the incorrect price and when I again unleashed the arsenal of the Word of God, the blood of Jesus and the name of Jesus against the spirit, she fled.

The Lord used this experience to teach me about how witches come against people in the nighttime because of an incident or an argument that occurred during the daytime. The spirits of offense and anger are dangerous.

The Holy Spirit Activates Your Spirit to Fight Witches at Night

When an assignment is sent against you, the witchcraft spirit will usually rise up to attack you between the hours of 12 midnight and 5 a.m. because they have to get back into their bodies before dawn. The way they operate is to press the person on his or her bed or come into the room as a shadowy figure with evil intentions. If the person studies the Word of God regularly, the Holy Spirit will use the Word to activate the person's spirit to rise up and quote the Word of God against the witch or wizard. In other words, as a **benefit of the Holy Spirit dwelling in our human Spirit, He helps our human spirit to war on our behalf when we feed on the Word of God.** <u>This is one of the reasons why Christians sometimes wake up just in time to see that their spirit is quoting the Word of God against an entity or rebuking something</u>.

<u>On the other hand, if a person has not been spending much time in the Word of God, he or she cannot move or even say the name of Jesus when the witches come to press him or her on the bed</u>. **The reason for this is because the person has not prepared his or her human spirit by the Word of God. Therefore, the Holy Spirit cannot use the Word to activate their human spirit.** Without the help of the Holy Spirit that dwells in our human spirit, the body is just clay and it feels like a log of wood that cannot move when left alone to fight demons. **It is our spirit that rises up to fight by the power of the Holy Spirit with the Word of God.** It rises above the body to war on our behalf. This is why the Lord said the following in **John 6:63:**

> "**It is the spirit that quickeneth;** the flesh profiteth **nothing:** <u>the words that I speak unto you</u>, they are **spirit**, and they are **life**."

The Word of God is our daily bread; it is spirit and it is our life. Therefore, we cannot afford to be low on the storage of the Word of God in our human spirit.

A Vision of How Our Spirit Fights

In the first couple of years of my becoming 'born again', the Lord showed me my human spirit. In this vision, I saw my spirit who was about 2 years old in the Lord at the time, flying in the face of the devil in a very bold and fierce manner. I watched as it was quoting the scripture saying, "It is written, **I will build my church and the gates of hell shall Never, Never, Never prevail against it!** I was amazed that my spirit was not only quoting the Word of God but had also written them out on the ground and was underlining the words **Never, Never, Never** over and over again with the finger! I was in awe at how my spirit that was less than 3 years old at the time was flying in the face of the devil that looked so much bigger.

When I woke up, I realized that the Lord had given me a very fierce warrior spirit; a fighting spirit but I learned that I have to feed it with the Word of God constantly because that is what it fights with. If you let your human spirit become anemic (deficient of the Word of God), when the witches are pressing you on your bed, it cannot rise. This is why you cannot only do your Bible study in the car on your way to work or on the run. You need to spend time in the Bible to put the Word of God in your spirit so that when a witchcraft assignment is sent against you, the Holy Spirit will use it to activate your spirit to fight on your behalf. We must not forget that there are wicked spirits out there and they are very active; they go on assignment against people in the nighttime. Therefore, we must walk daily according to **1 Peter 5:8-9:**

> **"Be sober, be vigilant; because your adversary the devil, as a roaring lion, walketh about, seeking whom he may devour:** 9 Whom resist stedfast in the faith, knowing that the same afflictions are accomplished in your brethren that are in the world."

Chapter 13
How to Overcome the Witchcraft Spirit

Avoid Rebellion against God: Be 'Born Again'

What gives the devil legal rights over people is the covenant that Adam made with him on behalf of humanity and this covenant brought spiritual death (separation from God) to humanity. **Being 'born again' in Christ Jesus brings spiritual life (reconnection with God) but anyone who chooses to remain in the Adamic Covenant with the devil, will continue to be the property of the devil.** The covenant with the devil becomes <u>null</u> and <u>void</u> in the life of everyone who is 'born again'. Being 'born again' also becomes a public declaration that you choose to belong to God instead of the devil and that you allow God to now legally protect you from the devil's wicked devices through the witchcraft spirit. This is why the Lord Jesus said the following in **John 3:3-8:**

> "...**Verily, verily, I say unto thee, Except a man be 'born again', he cannot <u>see</u> the kingdom of God.** *4* Nicodemus saith unto him, How can a man be born when he is old? can he enter the second time into his mother's womb, and be born? *5* Jesus answered, **Verily, verily, I say unto thee, Except a man be born of water and of the Spirit, he cannot <u>enter</u> into the kingdom of God.**
>
> *6* **That which is born of the flesh is flesh; and that which is born of the Spirit is spirit.** *7* Marvel not that I said unto thee, **Ye must be 'born again'.** *8* <u>The wind bloweth where it listeth, and thou hearest the sound thereof, but canst not tell whence it cometh, and whither it goeth:</u> **so is every one that is born of the Spirit.**"

It is very important for <u>all those who want to go to heaven</u> to ask the Lord Jesus to become the LORD of their lives and

to commit every area of their lives to Him forever. <u>He is the only one that can give us victory over the witchcraft spirit and He does this by giving us the 'Gift' of the **Holy Spirit** to keep us forever.</u> Therefore, make sure that you are Spirit-filled because the Bible tells us in **Romans 8:8-11** that if you do not have the <u>Spirit of Christ</u> **(the Holy Spirit)**, <u>you do not belong to Christ</u>:

> "So then they that are in the flesh cannot please God. 9 But ye are not in the flesh, but in the Spirit, if so be that the Spirit of God dwell in you. **Now if any man <u>have not the Spirit of Christ, he is none of his.</u>** 10 And if Christ be in you, the body is dead because of sin; but the Spirit is life because of righteousness. 11 But if the Spirit of him that raised up Jesus from the dead dwell in you, he that raised up Christ from the dead shall also quicken your mortal bodies by his Spirit that dwelleth in you."

As a 'born again' Christian, declare that your **New Covenant** by the blood of Jesus now covers every area of your life from witchcraft activities and assignments. Witches fear the blood of Christ, so invoke it often.

Be Grounded in the Word of God

Choose the Word of God and live by it. As a Christian, you cannot just have a head knowledge of what the Bible says but you must study it to get spiritual revelations from the Holy Spirit. **It is when the Word of God becomes a revelation to you that you can speak it effectively in faith.** In other words, do what the Bible tells us in **2 Timothy 2:15:**

> "Study to shew thyself approved unto God, a workman that needeth not to be ashamed, rightly dividing the word of truth."

The devil and his demons fear the Word of God because it is a spiritual sharp sword that cuts them to pieces if they disobey when it is issued as an order to them in the name of Jesus. No witch or a wizard can withstand the Word of God. Therefore, be grounded in the Word of God and do not seek after extra biblical teachings that challenge or contradict it. In other words, avoid having itching ears as stated **in 2 Timothy 4:3-4** because they attract demonic forces of which the witchcraft spirit is one:

> **"For the time will come when they will not endure sound doctrine; but after their own lusts shall they heap to themselves teachers, <u>having itching ears;</u>** 4 And they shall turn away their ears from the truth, and shall be turned unto fables."

There are people who always want to hear the new thing or the new revelation. According to the Apostle Paul, when you have itchy ears (wanting to hear something new all the time), you will fall into fables just like the Athenians. The Athenians were known for wanting to hear a new doctrine or a new thing all the time. Today, there are some preachers who fall into heresies because they think they have to pull out <u>a new revelation</u> as a magician pulls a trick from a hat. **The next thing you know, they start preaching heresies because they think that they are coming up with some <u>fantastic new revelation.</u>**

For example, there is a well-known minister in New York that was preaching that the reason that the black community has not been able to achieve respectability and financial success was because <u>it has not gone into the heart of darkness like the Italian mobs</u> did in their community to dominate that realm. According to him, once the Italian mobs began to dominate the dark realms to become the mob lords, they then began to see the loot manifest in the physical realm! This type of preaching is straight out the pit of hell and he has a well-known church in New York. We are not like the Italian mobs because the weapons of our warfare are not carnal (2 Corinthians 10:4). The Word of God is more powerful than guns and knives. We definitely do not need to be ruthless in killing people to rule or control them. We are called to set people free from such things.

These are the type of preachers who will bring the witchdoctors from Africa because they are looking for the spectacular and do not really care how they get it. We are to be vigilant because the Lord Jesus said that we will know the truth and the truth will make us free. You must believe that the Word of God is sufficient to produce your miracles, signs and wonders, healings and everything else that you need. Therefore, know the Word of God and avoid the works of the flesh as we saw in the scriptures.

Repent of Ancestral or Generational Witchcraft Covenants

To overcome the witchcraft spirit, you have to repent and renounce all the covenants that were made by you and the generations before you with the spirit. Also, you need to withdraw every invitation that you or the previous generations before you gave to the spirit into your bloodline. **As you have read so far, the witchcraft spirit has so many avenues of getting into a person's bloodline and even through the very education that people pride themselves in.** Ask God for forgiveness and cleansing from all witchcraft activities in your bloodline so that the blood of Jesus can cleanse and protect you. When we repent, God forgives us as stated in **1 John 1:8-9:**

> "If we say that we have no sin, we deceive ourselves, and the truth is not in us. 9 **If we confess our sins, he is faithful and just to forgive us our sins, and to cleanse us from all unrighteousness.**"

Declare your stand or believe that the practice of witchcraft is an abomination to you and verbally declare that you place the Cross of Jesus between you and all members of your family;

past and present as well as any of your acquaintances who are currently practicing witchcraft. Do this before praying so that your prayers will be effective.

Have an Active Prayer and Fasting Life

A very powerful weapon against the devil is fasting and praying. Prayers keep the witchcraft spirit away. The Word of God tells us in **James 5:16** that:

> "Confess your faults one to another, and pray one for another, that ye may be healed. **The effectual fervent prayer of a righteous man availeth much**."

Prayer ushers in the presence of God and the devil cannot abide where God's presence is. Therefore, you can drive away the witchcraft spirit by just your simple act of praying. **Prayers invite heaven to come into partnership with you as you bring your petitions before God.** It also keeps you from being anxious because you can release your burdens to God as you pray. He then helps you to think upon the things that are honest, true, just, etc., as outlined in **Philippians 4:6-8:**

> "**Be careful for nothing; but in everything by prayer and supplication with thanksgiving let your requests be made known unto God.** 7 And the peace of God, which passeth all understanding, shall keep your hearts and minds through Christ Jesus. 8 Finally, brethren, whatsoever things are true, whatsoever things are honest, whatsoever things are just, whatsoever things are pure, whatsoever things are lovely, whatsoever things are of good report; if there be any virtue, and if there be any praise, **think on these things**."

The Holy Spirit is truly our Helper and our Comforter because He helps us overcome difficult situations when we pray and when we fast. In order to avoid always having to pray against the witchcraft spirit, be sure to repent and renounce the covenants with it in your life and in your bloodline before praying. Also, revoke the invitation that was given to it against you.

Affirm Your New Bloodline and Heritage in Christ

As 'born again' Christians, the **Lord Jesus Christ is now** our **heritage** and our **lineage** because we are now **born of the Spirit of God**; we are born from on high. This is why we are called a <u>new creature</u> or <u>new creation</u> in **2 Corinthians 5:17-18:**

> "**Therefore if any man be in Christ, he is a** <u>**new creature**</u>**: old things are passed away; behold, all things are become new.** *18* And **all things are of God** *(we are now of God)*, who hath reconciled us to himself by Jesus Christ, and hath given to us the ministry of reconciliation."

And also in **Galatians 2: 20:**

> "**I am crucified with Christ: nevertheless I live; yet not I,** <u>**but Christ liveth in me:**</u> and the life which I now live in the flesh I live by the faith of the Son of God, who loved me, and gave himself for me."

As you affirm this **new creation** that **you now are**, you are setting yourself above your natural bloodline because the **new creation in Christ is from above**; from heaven! Basically, you are declaring that the 'old bloodline' and the 'old man' have passed away from your life and as a result, you are shutting the doors that they had provided for the witchcraft spirit to oppress you. <u>This is why my constant confession is that</u>: The **'me'** that my father and mother gave birth to was crucified with Christ and the **'me'** that now lives, is born of the Spirit of God; I am now from heaven above!

As new creations in Christ, we have now transcended all the evil and afflictions that were in our natural bloodline

but we must <u>believe</u> and <u>confess</u> it for it to work in our lives. Yes, you are a **new creation** even if you do not look like you have changed in the physical. Just because you still have the same body does not mean that you are not a **new creation** on the inside. You are brand new in God's book because you are 'born again' by His spirit and you have overcome every evil spirit in the world, above it and under it:

> **"For whatsoever is born of God overcometh the world:** and this is the victory that overcometh the world, even our faith. 5 **Who is he that overcometh the world, but he that believeth that Jesus is the Son of God?** 6 This is he that came by water and blood, even Jesus Christ; not by water only, but by water and blood. And it is the Spirit that beareth witness, because the Spirit is truth" (1 John 5:4-6).

Use the Name of Jesus

Concerning the power in the name of Jesus, I wrote the following in one of my books titled, ***How to Discern and Expel Evil Spirits***, *Chapter 6.* I think that it will be helpful to you:

*"**Rule #5: Pray with the Name of Jesus.***
*Another tool you can use to cast out demons is the use of the Name of Jesus. The Lord Himself gave us the legal authority and power to cast out unclean spirits or devils in His Name. He said in **Mark 16:17:***

> *'**And these signs shall follow them that believe; In my name shall they cast out devils; they shall speak with new tongues.**'*

*So, be bold to cast out devils in the name of the Lord Jesus. And also in **John 14:14:***

> *'**If ye shall ask any thing in my name, I will do it.**'*

*The Lord Jesus is the very authority that is backing us when we speak the Word of God and when we use His name. **I say to***

*you, that the Name of Jesus is heaven's valid currency.
It produces results. We are to use the Name of Jesus to enforce
the Kingdom of God on earth so that God's will can be done
on earth as it is in heaven. The Lord Jesus is in heaven but
we the believers (His body) are on earth.* **We are to enforce
His kingdom rule and dominion here on earth and we
are to do it in His Name.** *All of heaven backs the Name of
Jesus. God also commanded everything in heaven, on earth
and under the earth (which is the realm of evil spirits) to bow
at the mention of the Name of the Lord Jesus. We see this in*
Philippians 2:10-11:

> **'That at the name of Jesus every knee should bow,
> of things in heaven, and things in earth, and things
> under the earth; 11 And that every tongue should
> confess that Jesus Christ is Lord, to the glory of
> God the Father.'**

**All of heaven's arsenal is ready to punish and destroy
any evil spirit that does not obey any command that
you issue in the Name of Jesus and in faith..."**

The Name of Jesus in Blood on Our Foreheads

Concerning the blood of Jesus and as a 'born again'
Christian, God puts His seal on us; He seals us with the
name of His Son! In other words, we have the word **JESUS**
boldly written on our foreheads by His own finger and in
His blood! **It was an amazing sight to behold because it
repels, blinds and torments demons so that they cannot
stay around us.** This is why when you are dealing with
witchcraft spirit and its activities, you need to sing a lot
about the blood of Jesus that covers you; especially if you
are trying to pray and they are trying to contend for your
attention with strange footsteps, sounds or things that start
to fall down in your house or your room.

Just sing about the power of the blood of Jesus and how
you are covered by it in order to root them out. As for me,
when I go to a place and I am feeling oppressed, I just start

to softly sing, *"I am covered, I am covered, I am covered by the blood of Jesus"* and the demons will immediately take off. Try it the next time you are feeling oppressed in a place and you will be surprised at how quickly the atmosphere becomes calm. The devils do not like to hear the mention of the blood of Jesus. That is why the Bible says is **Revelation 12:11:**

> "And <u>they overcame him by the blood of the Lamb,</u> and <u>by the word of their testimony;</u> and they loved not their lives unto the death."

Avoid the Works of the Flesh

According to **Galatians 5:19-21**, the practice of witchcraft is listed as one of the works of flesh that will lead a person to hell and destruction:

> "Now the works of the flesh are manifest, which are these; <u>Adultery, fornication, uncleanness, lasciviousness,</u> 20 <u>Idolatry,</u> **witchcraft**, <u>hatred, variance, emulations, wrath, strife, seditions, heresies,</u> 21 <u>Envyings, murders, drunkenness, revellings,</u> and such like: of the which I tell you before, as I have also told you in time past, that **they which do such things shall not inherit the kingdom of God.**"

No one who practices any form of witchcraft shall inherit the kingdom of God. **In other words, no one who practiced witchcraft shall go to heaven unless he or she repents after accepting the Lord Jesus.** Witchcraft is a tool that the devil uses to get people to choose hell and destruction. Make the elimination of witchcraft practice something that you need to do in your life so that you can make heaven.

Not only do you want to avoid the works of the flesh, you also want to 'walk in the spirit'. This means that you have to purpose to know people, places and things by the Holy Spirit. **I never claim to know anyone until the Holy Spirit reveals**

the person to me because it is deceptive to know people by the flesh only. Anyone can come before you laughing and smiling with you but it takes the Holy Spirit to discern the spirit in the person. This is critical for those who are trying to choose a spouse; you cannot go by sight only:

> **"Wherefore henceforth know we no man after the flesh: yea, though we have known Christ after the flesh, yet now henceforth know we him no more"** (2 Corinthians 5:16).

Avoid Evil Gifts

Do not send gifts to people you know are into witchcrafts or demonic activities because they might use them as a point of contact to reach you. If you know that someone is into witchcraft, do not receive gifts from the person and do not give gifts or any of your personal items of clothing to the person. You do not have to be suspicious of people but listen to the Holy Spirit concerning giving and receiving from people that you suspect are into witchcraft. **You need to be balance in your discernment because suspecting everyone of witchcraft will make your life miserable; so what you need is to let the wisdom from the Holy Spirit guide you.**

This is why we are told to test every spirit that we encounter in people by the Spirit of God. **This does not mean that you have to refuse what people give you but rather, when you receive a gift from someone and all of a sudden you cannot sleep or are getting sick, you should be willing to get rid of it when the Holy Spirit highlights it as an evil gift.** Remember, all souls belong to God so all gifts are not bad; just the ones that have witchcraft attached to them.

Avoid Playful Activities that are Evil

I learned this lesson the hard way because I did not recognize that some playful activities can be evil. This was how I found out about this particular seemingly harmless one. One day, I went with someone to the store to shop for an electronic item. Since I was not buying any electronics, I volunteered to help her watch her little girl. As I played with the little girl, I noticed that there was a copy machine in the store that was plugged on so I took the little girl and went over to the copy machine. **We took turns in coping our palms.**

Afterwards, I took some of my photocopies home and the little girl took hers home with her mother but that night, the photocopies of my palm unleashed the psychic spirit against me! I watched as the spirit was trying to use my palm print as a way into my bedroom. **To me, it was just an innocent playtime with the little girl and I never thought about it as having any spiritual consequences.** As I was warring against the spirit, the Lord said to me, "Remember when you were in New York and how you gave your palm to a psychic to read?"

It was then that I remembered that about two <u>weeks after</u> I became 'born again', I was having my hair done when one of the hairdresser's clients came in. The hairdresser informed me that the lady was a psychic and she asked to read my palm. I thought it was childish but I went along with it and let her read my palm. Well, the spirit that rose up against me in my bedroom began using the photocopy of my palm to connect me to the psychic lady that read my palm in New York years ago! I repented for letting the psychic lady read my palm and I tore up the photocopies of my palm. I also renounced and came out of agreement with psychic spirit and it went away. This is just an example of the little things that the devil sees and uses as doors against people.

Summary of Ways to Overcome the Witchcraft Spirit

- Not working in rebellion to the Word of God
- Walking in love
- Walking in forgiveness
- Genuine happiness for those who are blessed
- Avoiding envy, jealousy, resentment and covetousness

- Not seeking revenge or retaliation but giving all revenge and retaliation over to the Lord
- Praying and fasting
- Using the name of Jesus
- Using the blood of Jesus

Conclusion

I hope that this book opened your eyes to the workings of the witchcraft spirit and how it adapts itself to various societies in different nations; including Western nations. I also hope that you paid particular attention to the things that attract and repel the spirit. In their quest for supernatural power and strange knowledge, many people have compromised the state of their souls by joining satanic organizations.

If your desire is for supernatural power, seek it only from the Lord and strive to **manifest the Fruits of the Holy Spirit** as stated in **Galatians 5:22-23**. The reason as you saw in this book is because no matter what 'power' the devil gives a person to control certain events, to 'heal', to 'cure', to become famous or to be rich, the end of it all is death. All the devil's agents that do not repent and seek Christ before they die shall perish. But the power that we receive from the Holy Spirit produces life and the fruit of the Spirit:

> "But the fruit of the Spirit is **love, joy, peace, longsuffering, gentleness, goodness, faith,** 23 **Meekness, temperance**: against such there is no law."

Being led by the Holy Spirit and seeking to manifest the fruit of the spirit is the only way that we can stay grounded in the ways of the Lord because the ways of the devil are very seductive but their end is eternal damnation.

The Lord Jesus has already bequeathed true spiritual powers to all those who belong to Him as stated in **Luke 10:19**:

> "**Behold, I give unto you power to tread on serpents and scorpions, and over all the power of the enemy: and nothing shall by any means hurt you.**"

All you need to do to receive this power is choose Jesus as your Lord and Savior by confessing Him as outlined below but your primary goal should be the salvation of your soul. He gives you power when you truly belong to Him.

Prayer to Make Jesus the Lord of Your Life:

"Lord Jesus, I believe with all my heart and I confess with my mouth that You are the Son of God and that You came into this world as God's lamb. You died on the Cross for my sins and You were buried. On the 3rd day, God the Father raised You up from the dead. Lord Jesus, come into my heart and be my Lord. I repent of all my sins including witchcraft. I ask You to forgive me and use Your blood to wash away all my sins including witchcraft from me and my bloodline.

I turn my life over to You to lead and guide me with Your Word. Also, I ask that You baptize me with the Holy Spirit to keep me, teach me the Bible and help me live my life for You. I choose to forsake all other religions and follow You as the only true way to God (John 14:6). Amen."

—Dr. Mary J. Ogenaarekhua

Appendix A
Prominent Occults and Secret Societies in the United States

Secret societies are organizations whose activities are hidden from people that are nonmembers. These activities are very demonic in nature hence there is a need for secrecy concerning them. The most prominent secret societies in this country today and in other Western nations are:

- **The Illuminates:** It was founded in 1776 in Ingolstadt (Upper Bavaria), by Adam Weishaupt. Its members are usually humanists and <u>their goal is to overthrow organized religion</u>. They are active in this country.

- **Freemasonry:** The Grand Masonic Lodge was formed in 1717. Their meetings involve demonic rituals and practices. It is a worldwide organization. Their members have to advance from one 'degree' to another in their quest for **'enlightenment'**. **These rituals are borrowed from the Egyptian cult of Isis and Horus hence the use of the Egyptian obelisk and pyramid with the 'eye of Horus'.** They use or make references to architectural symbols such as the compass and the square. It is an occultic organization and at the end of its last 'degrees' is pure satanic worship. New members are purposely deceived concerning the true nature of the organization until they get to a certain 'degree'.

- **Skull and Bones:** It was formed at Yale University in 1832 and only a few elites were allowed to become members. It is also known as the **Brotherhood of Death**. It is one of the oldest student secret societies in the United State and even to date, it uses masonic inspired rituals.

- **Order of the Garter:** It was founded by King Edward III and it is considered the most prestigious secret society in Europe. It is in honor of St. George, the patron saint of England. According to Wikipedia, **"Membership of the Order is limited to the Sovereign, the Prince of Wales and no more than 24 members, or companions."** The order also includes knights and ladies (e.g. members of the British Royal Family and foreign monarchs). New appointments to the Order of the Garter are always announced on St. George's Day, 23 April as Saint George is the patron saint of England." It is depicted in the Royal Coats of Arms. It is highly demonic.

- **Rosicrucianism:** It was found in Germany in 1378 by a man named **Christian Rosenkreuz** or 'Rose-cross'. According to Wikipedia, "It holds a doctrine or theology 'built on esoteric truths of the ancient past' which 'concealed from the average man, provide insight into nature; the physical universe and the spiritual realm.' It is symbolized by the 'Rosy Cross'. It is a worldwide organization and its members practice occultic rituals, transcendental meditation and astra projection. It is the forerunner of the Order of the Golden Dawn.

- **Order of the Golden Dawn:** It was created by Dr. William Robert Woodman, William Wynn Westcott and Samuel Liddell MacGregor Mathers. The three of them were also members of the Rosicrucian society in Anglia (an organization with ties to Freemasonry). Many people consider the **Golden Dawn** to be a forerunner of the **Ordo Templi Orientis** and a majority of modern Occult groups.

- **Ordo Templis Orentis:** It is a mystic organization of the early twentieth century and their practices were similar to those of the Freemasons. They also use ritual and occultic practices to graduate their members from one level of elevation to another. **They believe in the new age self-promoted doctrines and practices as a way of arriving at one's true identity.** The group's beliefs and practices were composed by the well-known satanist called **Aleister Crowley** who is famous for creating the **New Age Movement**. He became the leader of the group and he developed the group's manifesto called the <u>Mysteria Mystica Maxima</u>.

- **Knights Templar:** Its full name is: The United Religious, Military and Masonic Orders of the Temple and of St John of Jerusalem, Palestine, Rhodes and Malta. It is a modern off-shoot of Freemason and **its practices are different from the medieval old order of the Knights Templar of the 12th century**. It is a glamourized higher degree of Freemason but it uses the pumps and decorations of the 12th century Knights Templar.

- **Eckankar:** It is a secret society founded with headquarters in Chanhassen, Minnesota. **Its followers believe in an "individual spiritual path to an understanding of self as eternal soul and the development of higher states of consciousness."** The members refer to themselves as **Eckists**. Just like the Rosicrucians, Eckists practice transcendental meditation and Astra Projection.

- **Druids:** The druids are the Celtic peoples of Gaul, Britain, Ireland and other groups of the Iron Age. Their religious activities were known to be highly demonic because they included the performance of both animal and human sacrifices. They also believed in reincarnation and practiced sorcery.

- **Norse Mythology:** This is the mythology of the North Germanic people which are based on Norse paganism. Even after the advent of Christianity, they are still woven into the Scandinavian folklore of today. The Norse mythology is made up of tales of different deities, heroes and beings from medieval manuscripts, archaeological representations and folk traditions.

- **Bohemian Grove:** Bohemian Grove is a 2,700-acre campground located at 20601 Bohemian Avenue, Monte Rio, California. It is owned by a private San Francisco-based **Men's Art Club** popularly known as **the Bohemian Club.** The Bohemian Club is an all-male club and its membership and guest list includes musicians, artists as well as many prominent business leaders. There are also government officials (including U.S. presidents), senior media executives, and people of power. <u>At the Bohemian Grove and in mid-July of each year, there is a two-week, three-weekend camping of some of the most powerful men in the world</u>. At this event is what they call the **'burning of care'**.

This is a satanic ritual in which the people turn in 'all their worldly cares' and they are made into an effigy that looks like a baby. The effigy is placed on the altar (a slab) carved out of the belly **a giant owl** made of stone; complete with fireworks and loud speakers. Yes, the owl speaks to all in attendance. The ceremonial members dress up in their satanic outfits and march in a procession towards the altar of the owl. As the procession is going on, the owl begins to speak with the voice of the late CBS anchorman Walter Cronkite. **They then sacrifice 'care' on the altar of the owl while fireworks are displayed like the fourth of July.** Heads of nations and prominent world leaders and business men attend this event.

Important political and business deals have been developed at the Grove. The Grove is particularly famous for a **Manhattan Project** planning meeting that took place there in September 1942 that <u>led to the development of the atomic bomb</u>. Those attending this meeting included Ernest Lawrence, U.C. Berkeley colleague Robert Oppenheimer, various military officials, the S-1 Committee heads such as the presidents of Harvard, Yale and Princeton along with representatives of Standard Oil and General Electric *(source: Wikipedia)*.

The one thing that the above secret societies have in common is that they are all demonic and they are all witchcraft organizations that are involved in the worship of satan. Any Christian who was formerly a member of any of these secret societies above or any other ones needs to repent and renounce their involvement so that God can shut their doors in his or her life.

Appendix B
Satanic Crimes around the World

The following are summarized news accounts of satanic crimes from around the world. The practice of witchcraft is a global problem but as I stated before, the witchcraft spirit adapts itself to the various cultures around the world. Be not afraid of satan and all his agents because 'born again' believers have the power to pray them away and destroy all their works. To effectively do this, I have two prayer books that can help you overcome the devil's afflictions: **Effective Prayers for Various Situations Vol. 1 and Vol. 2.** These books are available at **www.maryjministries.org.**

Brasilla, Brazil – According to an international news agency, the stepfather of a 2-year-old boy along with a couple of other people were arrested after a toddler was discovered with 42 needles in his body (other news accounts say it was about 50 needles). The reports said that some of them were about two inches long. The stepfather admitted to sticking the boy with the needles as part of a **'Santeria-like ritual'.** According to the Brazilian police, the stepfather said that "a woman who went into a trance commanded him to stick the needles in the boy's body." **Santeria** is called Macumba in Brazil and it is like the Santeria that those in Cuba, Puerto Rico and Miami practice. There is also the practice a 'black magic version' of Santeria called Quimbanda or Zarabanda in Brazil. **The report stated that the boy's father told the newspapers that he believed his son was the victim of a 'black magic ritual'.**

Western Russia: According to one of UK's popular newspapers, authorities in Western Russia arrested a group of teenagers belonging to a satanists cult "for sacrificing and eating their victim's remains in a 'cannibal feast'. The teenagers were all charged with homicides. They were accused of killing and eating a total of four victims! According to the teachers of the accused, they have "lower than average intelligence, moody and Goths." The report stated that every one of the victims was "stabbed 666 times before being roasted in a bonfire." The charred remains of the victims were found in a pit in a wooded area and they also found an upside down cross with a rat crucified on it over the pit.

Police have been looking for the missing victims for months before the discovery. The father of one of the victims informed the police that his son told him that he "had satanists among friends" and that he was not afraid to be with them. At the time, his father did not think that any harm will come to his son by him just sitting with a bunch of satanists in a cemetery. **After the arrest, the head of the satanic cult told police authority that "the reason he became a satanist was because God didn't make him rich" but that things changed or got better "when he prayed to the devil."** His quest for riches led him into cannibalism.

Deltona, Florida: According to a newspaper in Orlando, a picture of the Deltona Commissioner was found glued to a voodoo doll and placed in the front yard of her home. The report stated that there were pins on the head, body and legs of the doll. As a result, the city is now requiring extra security for the Commissioner and other city leaders. When the Commissioner saw the 6-inch doll, she said, "My first thought was somebody wants to destroy me." She further elaborated by saying, "I don't know a lot about these things, but because of all the pins, I assume someone wants me destroyed." **According to the report, Deltona is very close** to Cassadaga; the **"tiny village of psychics and occultic bookstores is a magnet for occultic 'wierdos' of all kinds."** Another national news agency stated that "Cassadaga is considered the last of two spiritualist camps in the U.S."

Mzuzu, Malawi: According to an international news agency, the Malawi police department dismantled a teenage satanic group practicing vampirism. The group's hidden identity was discovered when the members requested one of the teenage girls to kill her father. She went to her church and confessed her involvement and the request from the group to her pastor. The **police revealed that the girl also confessed to "sucking people's blood" and travelling frequently with her friends to take part in "meetings with their 'queen' in the Indian Ocean."** Two teenage girls were arrested by the Mzuzu police for "coercing a 14 year-old student into the satanic cult." The girls are likely to be charged and tried in the court of law.

Santa Maria, CA: According to a news agency in California, a Wiccan couple were arrested and charged with "lewd and lascivious acts with a minor." The police report states that the couple "used their Wicca religion to lure a 15-year-old girl into sex." They revealed that the couple used "wiccan rituals and other drugs to lure the teen. Their practices were centered on different types of sexual acts.

Saudi Arabia: According an Arabic news agency, an Egyptian man was executed after he was convicted of 'sorcery', desecrating the Koran and adultery. The man was "accused by another foreign resident of practicing magic in order to separate him from his wife." The authority said that they found evidence such as "books on black magic, a candle with an incantation 'to summon devils' and some foul-smelling herbs" in the man's house. They also stated that the man confessed to having been involved in adultery with a woman…

Bishkek, Kyrgyzstan: According to a popular Kyrgyzstan news agency, two people (a 16 year old and a 27 year old) held hands and jumped from a 12-story building to their death in a neighborhood called Vostok. The report stated that two other people had also jumped to their death in the same way just a few weeks before. In each of the cases, the police authority discovered satanic notebook on the scene. A witness identified the notebook as being about satan. Upon examination, the last page of the notebook instructed the members to "sacrifice" themselves to satan and it showed the signatures of the two people that jumped. They signed and dated the page before they jumped. The witness stated that, "first, they threw the notebook down and after that they jumped from the roof." Also, some people that live in the same neighborhood as the girls confirmed that the girls practiced satanism and that they even had satanic tattoos. Their coven had 14 members and was headed by a young man.

Glossary of Key Definitions

Monotheism: The belief that there is <u>only One God</u>.

Judaism: It is the religion, philosophy, and way of life of the Jewish people. It is the traditional Hebrew Bible that is also known as the **Tanakh** and it is also explored in later texts such as the **Talmud**. In essence, Judaism is the expression of the covenant relationship that God developed with the children of Israel. According to traditional Rabbinic Judaism, God revealed His Laws and Commandments to Moses on Mount Sinai in the form of both the <u>Written</u> and <u>Oral</u> **Torah**.

Christianity: The belief that God fulfilled His promise to send the Messiah to the Jewish people and to the world in the person of Jesus Christ as the only way out of sin. He came as the Savior of all of mankind and He is the only way to God. Those who believe in Him are called Christians because they believe that Jesus Christ is Anointed of God and that He is the fulfillment of all of God's righteous requirements written in the Law of Moses.

Polytheism: The belief in <u>more than one</u> God.

Pantheism: The belief or the view that the Universe (Nature) and God are identical.

Classical Pantheism: It <u>equates existence with God</u> and has an inclusive demeanor towards other world faiths. Meaning 'All-God' or 'All is God.'

Naturalistic Pantheism (also called scientific pantheism): It encompasses feelings of reverence towards nature and the wider universe. It embraces rationalism and the scientific method and **it affirms the <u>nonexistence</u> of supernatural realms, afterlives, beings or forces**.

Pandeism or Pan-Deism: It is from Ancient Greek and Latin (Dues): It incorporates elements of pantheism but believes that 'God' or its metaphysical equivalent is identical to the

Universe. **It believes that the Creator-God who designed the universe no longer exists in a status where it can be reached but instead <u>can be confirmed only by reason</u>.** Its essence is the belief that the Creator of the universe actually became the universe and so ceased to exist as a separate and conscious entity. Through this synergy pandeism claims to answer primary objections to deism; (why would God creates and then not interact with the universe?) and (how did the universe originate and what is its purpose?).

Gaia Philosophy (named after Gaia, Greek goddess of the Earth): Is a broadly inclusive term for related concepts that living organisms on a planet will affect the nature of their environment in order to make the environment more suitable for life. This set of theories holds that all organisms on an extraterrestrial life-giving planet regulate the biosphere to the benefit of the whole.

Gaia Hypothesis: It is the idea that we may have discovered a living being bigger; more ancient, and more complex than anything from our wildest dreams. That being, called Gaia, is **the Earth**.

Archaeoastronomy (also spelled archeoastronomy): Is the study of how people in the past "have understood the phenomena in the sky, how they used phenomena in the sky and what role the sky played in their cultures. **It uses other cultures' symbolically rich cultural interpretations to understand the phenomena in the sky**.

Astronomy: It is a natural science that deals with the study of celestial objects (such as stars, planets, comets, nebulae, star clusters and galaxies) and phenomena that originate outside the Earth's atmosphere (such as the cosmic background radiation).

Ecology (from Greek 'study of'): It is the scientific study of the relations that living organisms have with respect to each other and their natural environment.

Environmentalism: It is a broad philosophy and social movement regarding concerns for environmental conservation and improvement of the health of the environment, particularly as the measure for this health seeks to incorporate the concerns of non-human elements.

Psychology: It is the science of behavior and mental processes. Its immediate goal is to understand individuals and groups by both establishing general principles and researching specific cases.

Physics (from Ancient Greek 'nature'): It is a natural science that involves the study of matter and its motion through space-time, along with related concepts such as energy and force.

Buddhism: Teaching by **Siddhartha Gautama also known as Buddha** who shared his insights about awakening or enlightenment to help **sentient** beings end suffering (dukkha), achieve **nirvana** (a state of being free from suffering), and escape what is seen as a cycle of suffering and rebirth. **It is a religious belief with a main theme of reincarnation**.

Taoism: It is the consolidation of a number of concepts and practices that make up the 'Path' or 'Way' of living. The consolidation of ideas and concepts include basic principles or 'theories' regarding the body, diet, breathing and physical exercises, uses of herbs, philosophical inquiry and, of course, meditation. All of which the Taoist feels brings a human being into closer alignment with the 'natural order' of life and living. **Reverence for ancestral spirits and immortals are common in popular Taoism.** Organized Taoism distinguishes its ritual activity from that of the folk religion, which some professional Taoists (Dàoshi) view as debased.

Chinese Folk Religion or Chinese traditional religions is a collection of ethnic religious traditions which have been a main belief system in China and among Han Chinese ethnic groups.

Shenism comprises Chinese mythology and it includes the worship of shens 'deities', 'spirits', 'awarenesses', 'consciousnesses', and 'archetypes' which can be nature's deities, Taizu or clan deities, city deities, national deities, cultural heroes and demigods, dragons and ancestors.

Hinduism: Frequently expressed as meaning 'the eternal law', 'the eternal law that sustains, upholds and surely preserves' amongst many other expressions by its adherents. The 'power' that lies behind nature and that keeps everything in balance is a natural forerunner to the idea of Dharma. The idea of **rta** (natural order) laid the cornerstone of **dharma's** implicit attribution to the 'ultimate reality'. **They see Dharma as the universal principle of law, order, harmony, all-in-all truth that sprang first from <u>Brahman.</u>** According to this belief, **Brahman** is the holy or sacred power that is the source and sustainer of the universe.

Sikhism: It is a monotheistic religion founded in fifteenth century Punjab, India on the teachings of Guru Nanak Dev Ji and ten successive Sikh Gurus (the last teaching being the the text of Guru Granth Sahib Ji). The principal beliefs of Sikhism are **faith** and **justice**, in Waheguru — represented by the phrase **ik ōakār,** meaning one God. Sikhism advocates the pursuit of salvation through disciplined, personal meditation on the name and message of God. The followers of Sikhism are ordained to follow the teachings of the ten Sikh gurus, or 'enlightened leaders'.

Ouija Boards: It is spirit and fire key board or talking board. It is a flat board marked with the letters of the alphabet, the numbers 0-9, the words 'yes' 'no' 'hello' and 'goodbye', and other symbols and words are sometimes also added to help personalize the board. The word is supposed to be of French and German origin.

About the Author

I am a born again Christian who believes in the preservation of human life and the sanctity of marriage as defined by the Bible. I also believe in letting God set our agenda rather than us setting the agenda for Him. Below is the biographical information about me.

Biographical Information

Name: Prophetess Mary J. Ogenaarekhua, PhD (pronounced **Oge-nah-re-qua**).

Founder: Mary J. Ministries, Inc.; To His Glory Publishing Company, Inc.

Educational Background: BA Communications-Journalism, Masters Degree in Public Administration and a PhD in Theology

Dr. Mary Justina Ogenaarekhua was born in Nigeria. She grew up in a Muslim home with her grandparents and she attended Roman Catholic elementary and high schools. The Lord miraculously raised Mary up from the dead when she took a fatal fall in her early years. Prophetess Mary is gifted with the ability to heal the sick, to interpret visions and dreams, to hear the voice of the Lord, to discern spirits and to intercede as a mighty prayer warrior. Also, she is also the Lord's scribe.

Dr. Mary operates in the gift of prophecy with the ability to see into the spiritual realm. God has opened Prophetess Mary's spiritual eyes to see His desire for His people. She's a teacher of the unadulterated Word of God; a true woman of God in rare spiritual form! She holds workshops and conferences as well as teaches and preaches on many topics including **deliverance, healing, visions and dreams, spiritual discernment, understanding the power of covenants,**

effective prayers, mentoring, leadership training and much more. She conducts **evangelism and outdoor crusades internationally** with thousands in attendance.

Dr. Mary Justina Ogenaarekhua is the author of the following books:

(1) Unveiling the God-Mother. This book is a biography of *Mary's death and resurrection experience* and her early years in Africa. It details the spiritual events that happened to her before she became a Christian and before she came to the United States. She also discusses some of the events and holidays that a lot of Christians celebrate ignorantly.

(2) Keys to Understanding Your Visions and Dreams: A Classroom Approach. In this book about visions and dreams, she uses the Word of God to instruct the body of Christ on visions and dreams. She applies the first-hand revelation knowledge that she learned from the Lord Himself. This book is a must read for everyone who dreams and everyone who sees visions. It will teach you how to interpret both with the Word of God.

(3) A Teacher's Manual on Visions and Dreams. This manual is designed to teach the average person, bishops, pastors, etc., the basic principles about visions and dreams, about sources of vision and dreams, about identifying the sources of your visions and dreams and about analyzing their contents. It is meant to be used along with the above textbook titled, *Keys to Understanding Your Visions and Dreams*.

(4) How to Discern and Expel Evil Spirits. This is a very powerful book for all those who are called to the healing and deliverance ministry. In it, Dr. Mary answers the questions most people have concerning evil spirits, and she teaches on the origin of evil spirits, how to discern and expel them and she answers the question, "Can a Christian have a demon?" This is a foundational resource for all those who want to walk in great spiritual discernment and to cast out devils.

(5) A Teacher's Manual on Discerning and Expelling Evil Spirits. This is a powerful teacher's tool with a step by step teaching on key principles about evil spirits, the origin of evil spirits and how to identify and expel evil spirits. It is meant to be used along with the above textbook on *How to Discern and Expel Evil Spirits*. If your desire is to teach others, you can follow the teaching strategies outlined in this book.

(6) How I Heard from God: The Power of Personal Prophesy. Prophetess Mary Ogenaarekhua outlines key principles concerning personal prophecy and she lays out a blue print of what to do with your personal prophetic words. She helps the reader understand the conditions that are attached by God to every personal prophetic word. Failure to understand these conditions will keep your God-given prophetic word from coming to pass.

(7) Effective Prayers for Various Situations: Volumes I and II. In *Effective Prayers*, Prophetess Mary outlines principles on how to pray effectively concerning various life situations. Both of these books contain prayers for almost every situation that a lot of Christians battle with. Many have given testimonies about the deliverance and blessings manifested in their lives as a result of praying the prayers in these books.

(8) Keys to Successful Mentoring Relationships. In this book, Dr. Mary outlines the dynamics involved in a mentoring relationship and the actual steps and stages of mentoring. She also highlights the pitfalls to avoid.

(9) A Workbook for Successful Mentoring. This workbook is a powerful teaching guide for all those who want to be mentored and those who desire to mentor others. It is a teacher/student's valuable tool for teaching and practicing mentoring. It is meant to be used along with the above textbook titled, *Keys to Successful Mentoring Relationships.*

(10) Understanding the Power of Covenants. This book teaches on the power of covenants. Covenants impact our lives for good or for bad on a daily basis. It allows us to learn about how God uses covenants, how the devil uses covenants and how God wants us to use covenants so that we can receive what He has for us and avoid the devil's attempts to use negative covenants to hinder us. Negative covenants can hinder a person's progress throughout the person's life.

(11) Secrets About Writing and Publishing Your Book: What Other Publishers Will Not Tell You. This book is a powerful synopsis of what you need to know in order to write and get your book published and also how to position your book for mass marketing. It is designed to help all those who desire to write and market their books.

(12) The Agenda of the Few. This book is a call for the Church to get back to its God-given purpose for this country (USA); which is to reach all Americans for God. For too long now, the Church has been functioning as though it is only called to one political party –the Republican Party. The issues discussed in this book are meant to remind the reader that there are Ten Commandments in the Bible and that God can choose to address any of these commandments at any given time. Therefore, we must be willing to get the Church out of the Republican Party box that we have placed it in and learn to seek God's will during each presidential election. He is God of the Republicans, the Democrats and the Independents.

(13) The Agenda of the Masses. Just like the *"Agenda of the Few"* above that was written to the Christian Conservatives in the Republican Party, this book addresses what the Lord showed me that a lot of the <u>Christians in the Democratic Party</u> are doing that equally displeases Him. They have allowed a very large segment of the Church to be pulled away by 'the agenda of the masses.' In other words, they have bought into the ungodly doctrines, ideologies, beliefs, and political views of the masses to the point that now, their version of Christianity within the Democratic Party is essentially 'anything goes.' In their attempt <u>to please the masses</u>, they have embraced the pagan gods and have lumped their worship together with the worship of the Judeo-Christian God of the Bible.

(14) What Tribe of Israel Am I From? This book is designed to answer the questions of some Christians who are trying to determine the tribe of the <u>natural Israel</u> that they are from. The reason they want to know this is because there are some teachings going on in Christendom in which Christians are being assigned to the various tribes of Israel. This book will help anyone to determine the tribe of Israel that they are from. It is an eye-opener for anyone who desires to know the truth.

(15) Experiencing the Depths of God the Father. This book is the first in a series of three books titled, *Experiencing the Depths of God the Father, Experiencing the Depths of Jesus Christ,* and *Experiencing the Depths of the Holy Spirit.* It is written to help you know God in depth as well as understand the mysteries that He has coded in His Word for you. Therefore, this book is for you if you want to know God in a deeper way so that you can receive all that He has for you. It is truly a book for all those who want to know God in a deeper more intimate way.

(16) Experiencing the Depths of Jesus Christ. This book is written to help you know Jesus in depth and to know how <u>He existed in the spiritual realm</u> as well as <u>in the Old Testament</u> before He was manifested as the <u>Son of God</u> on earth. It is filled with revelation of who the Lord Jesus is and how He has been dealing with us since man fell into sin. You will be excited as you see the Lord Jesus revealed to you in a way that you have never known before.

(17) Experiencing the Depths of the Holy Spirit. God the Father and the Lord Jesus are both in heaven; it is the Holy Spirit that is here with us on earth and both the Father and the Lord Jesus relate to us through the Holy Spirit. Therefore, **we need to get to know Him better so that we can learn His ways and be better able to follow His leading and guidance.** This book is written to help you know Him in depths.

(18) How the Jezebel Spirit Operates and the Anointing that Destroys Her. This book will help the reader understand who the Jezebel spirit is and how to defeat her, what attracts her to a person and what repels her. You will also learn about her origin, tactics (through men and women) and how to arm yourself against her. **Many people wrestle with this spirit in their workplaces, in their marriages and in their inter-personal relationships.** This book will equip you so that you are able to both discern and expel her without falling into her ways.

Dr. Mary O. lives in Atlanta and is the founder of **Mary J. Ministries** and **To His Glory Publishing Company, Inc.** She is an ordained minister with a strong Deliverance Anointing. She has appeared on Trinity Broadcasting Network and other national television programs.

About Mary J. Ministries

Mary J. Ministries was founded by Dr. Mary J. Ogenaarekhua to equip and impart the anointing of God to the Body of Christ, for the purpose of impacting the whole world. Our goal is to help men, women, old and young to build relationships through Bible Studies, Community Outreach, Prayer Support, Caring Ministries, Teaching on Visions and Dreams, Discernment/Deliverance, Evangelism, Mentoring, Fellowship and Special Events.

As an ordained minister, Prophetess Mary O. teaches, trains and activates individuals to properly operate their prophetic gifts, discernment, deliverance and ministry outreach and interpretation of visions and dreams. Teachings provided by Prophetess Mary O. are inspired by God and are balanced biblical principles for the purpose of developing a spirit of excellence, wholeness and GODLY character.

Prophetess Mary O. is committed to helping the Body of Christ and those who do not yet know the Lord Jesus as their personal Savior to understand their God-given purpose. Mary J. Ministries regularly hosts classes, seminars, conferences and crusades in this nation as well as in other countries.

Mary J. Ministries
Phone: **770-458-7947**
Website: www.maryjministries.org

About To His Glory Publishing Co.

To His Glory Publishing Company, Inc. was also founded by Dr. Mary J. Ogenaarekhua to help writers become published authors. Our goal is to help new and established writers edit, publish and market their work for a reasonable cost.

To His Glory Publishing Company, Inc. offers one of the most cost effective and stress-free ways of getting a manuscript published.

Books published by To His Glory Publishing Company will be made available in most of the major on-line bookstores like Amazon.com, Barnes & Noble.com, Books-a-million.com, etc.

Our authors receive a 40% royalty on the net sales of their books! Upon request, we submit our published books for buyers and distributors such as Wal-Mart, Family Christian Bookstores, drugstores, Publix and Kroger for review and purchase for their chains of stores.

We are a Christian organization with the sole purpose of bringing glory to the name of our Lord Jesus Christ. Therefore, we will not publish obscene or offensive materials.

To His Glory Publishing Company, Inc. reserves the right to reject any manuscript it deems obscene or offensive.

To His Glory Publishing Company, Inc.
Phone: **770-458-7947**
Website: www.tohisglorypublishing.com

Bibliography

Diodorus, Siculus. *Bibliotheca Historica*, Greek historian of Agyrium in Sicily, ca. 80–20 BC, wrote <u>forty books</u> of world history called *Bibliotheca Historica* or *World History*, in three parts: mythical history of peoples, non-Greek, Greek and the Trojan War; history to Alexander's death (323 BC); history to 54 BC. From this are, Books I–V (Egyptians, Assyrians, Ethiopians, Greeks) and Books XI–XX (Greek history 480–302 BC). The Loeb Classical Library edition of Diodorus Siculus is in twelve volumes.

Ogenaarekhua, Mary J. *How the Jezebel Spirit Operates, and the Anointing that Destroys Her.* To His Glory Publishing Company, Lilburn, GA, USA, 2014.

Ogenaarekhua, Mary J. *How to Discern and expel Evil Spirit.* To His Glory Publishing Company, Lilburn, GA, USA, 2005.

Ogenaarekhua, Mary J. *Keys to Understanding Your Visions and Dreams.* To His Glory Publishing Company, Lilburn, GA, USA, 2004.

Ogenaarekhua, Mary J. *Understanding the Power of Covenants.* To His Glory Publishing Company, Lilburn, GA, USA, 2008.

Ogenaarekhua, Mary J. *Unveiling the God-mother.* To His Glory Publishing Company, Lilburn, GA, USA, 2003.

Wikipedia.com.

TO HIS GLORY PUBLISHING COMPANY, INC.

463 Dogwood Dr. Lilburn, GA. 30047, U.S.A (770)458-7947

Order Form for Bookstores in the USA

Order Date: _____

Order Placed By: _____   By Fax: _____

Address: _____
_____

City _____ ST/ZIP _____

Phone #: _____

Email: _____

Purchase Order#: _____

Return Policy: Within 1 year but not before 90 Days.

Price	Quantity	List Price
Shipping Method:		
Media:		
UPS:		
FedEx:		
Other (Please Specify):		
Total Price:	Total Quantity:	**List Price**

Ship To Address: Bill to Address:

Other Books by Prophetess Mary Ogenaarekhua

ISBN 978-0-9791566-8-7

ISBN 978-0-9821900-2-9

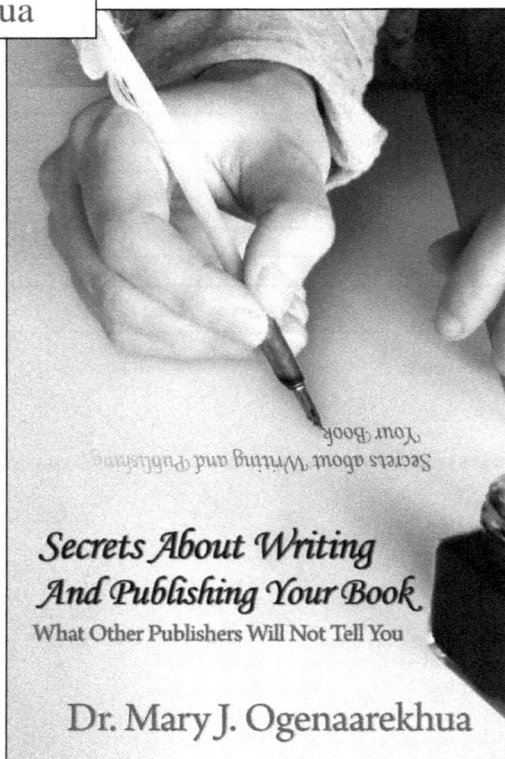

Other Books by Prophetess Mary Ogenaarekhua

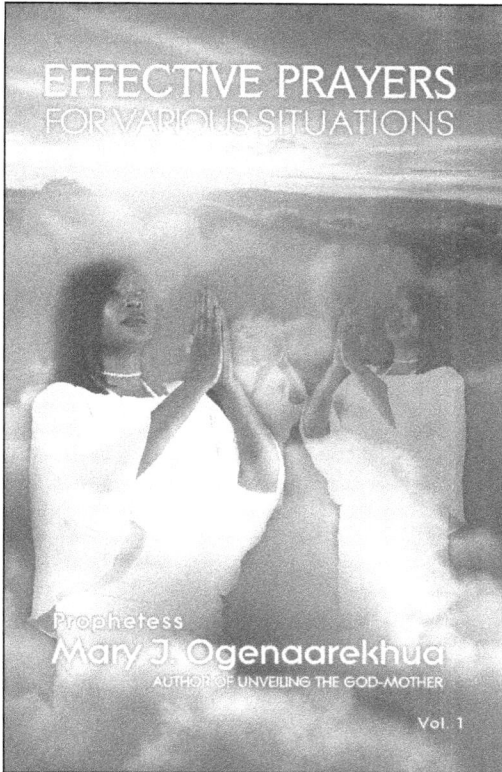

ISBN 978-0-9774265-6-0

ISBN 978-0-9774265-9-1

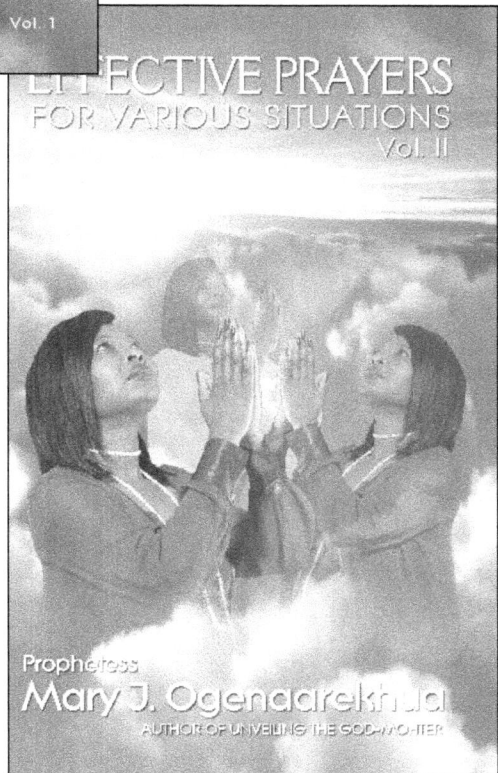

Other Books by Prophetess Mary Ogenaarekhua

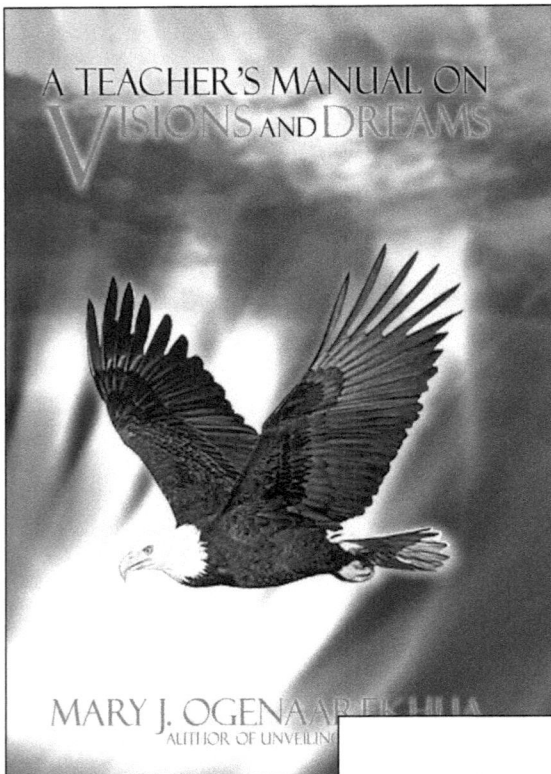

A TEACHER'S MANUAL ON VISIONS AND DREAMS

MARY J. OGENAAREKHUA
AUTHOR OF UNVEILING

ISBN 978-0-9749802-1-8

ISBN 978-0-9749802-8-7

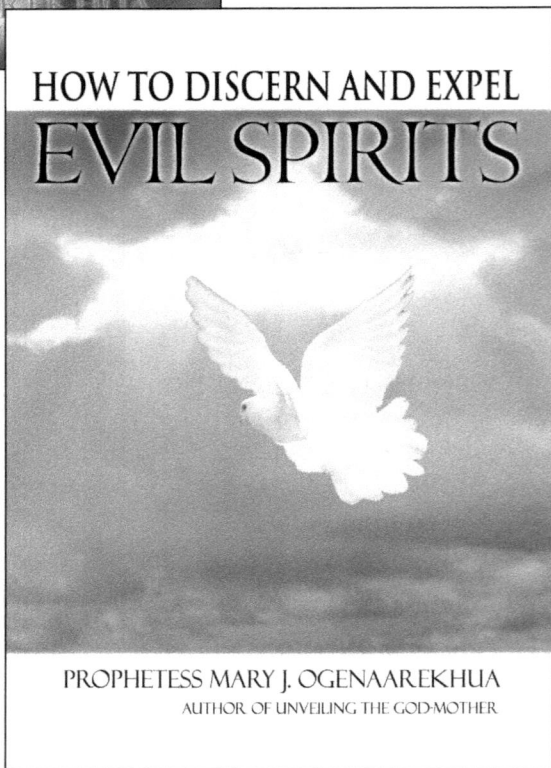

HOW TO DISCERN AND EXPEL EVIL SPIRITS

PROPHETESS MARY J. OGENAAREKHUA
AUTHOR OF UNVEILING THE GOD-MOTHER

Other Books by Prophetess Mary Ogenaarekhua

ISBN 978-0-9791566-6-3

ISBN 978-1-5873628-0-4

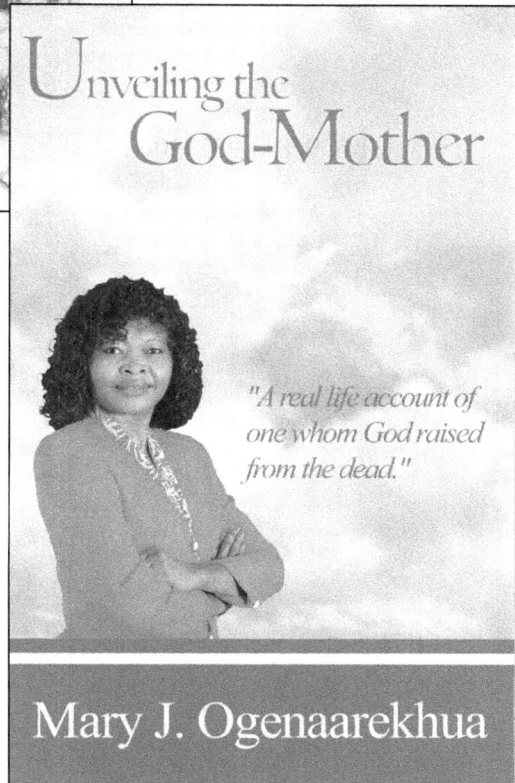

Other Books by Prophetess Mary Ogenaarekhua

ISBN 978-0-9821900-7-4

ISBN 978-0-9821900-8-1

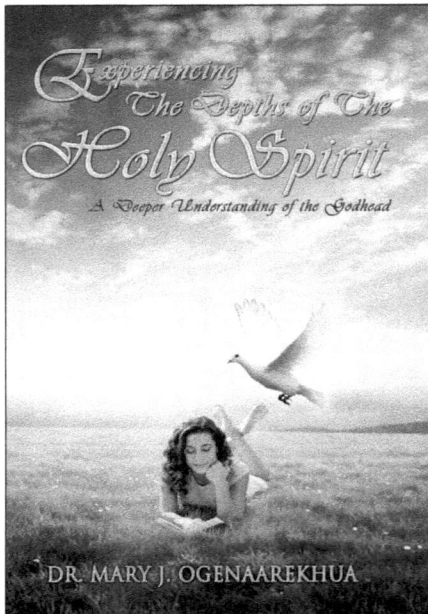

ISBN 978-0-9854992-2-8

Other Books by Prophetess Mary Ogenaarekhua

ISBN 978-1-5873628-0-4

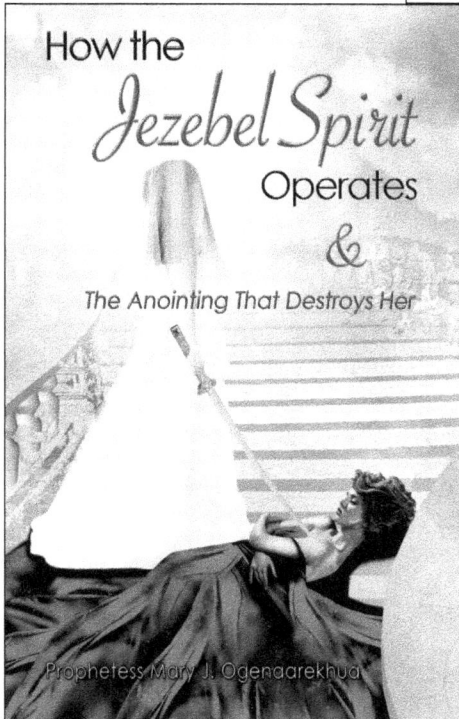

What Tribe of Israel Am I From?

Dr. Mary J. Ogenaarekhua

How the Jezebel Spirit Operates & The Anointing That Destroys Her

Prophetess Mary J. Ogenaarekhua

ISBN 978-0-9854992-6-6

Other Books by Prophetess Mary Ogenaarekhua

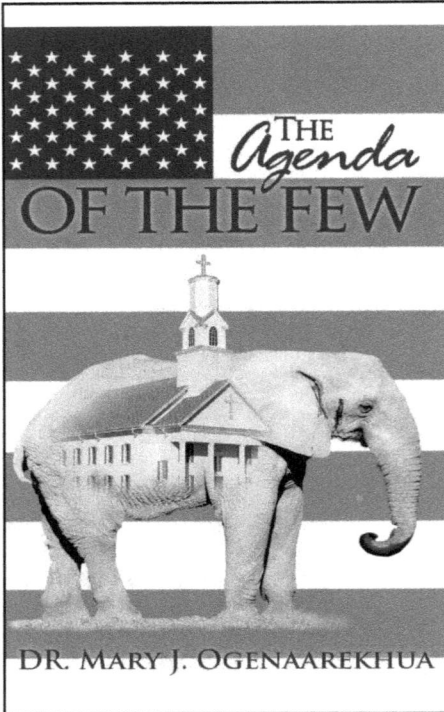

THE *Agenda* OF THE FEW

DR. MARY J. OGENAAREKHUA

ISBN 978-0-9821900-1-2

ISBN 978-0-9821900-4-3

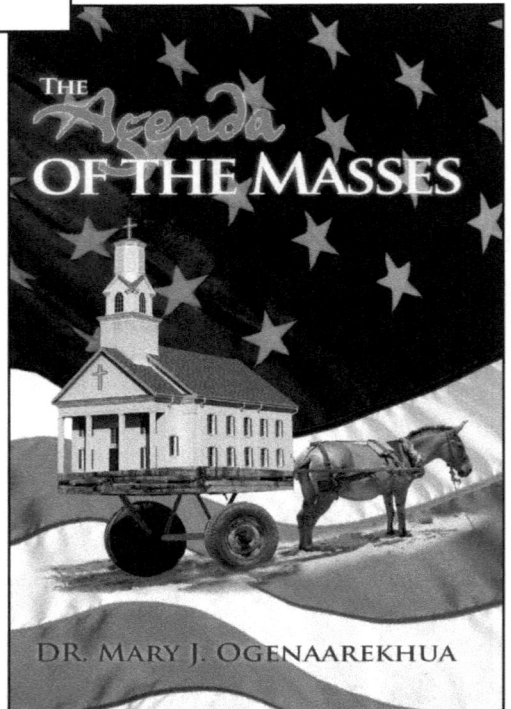

THE *Agenda* OF THE MASSES

DR. MARY J. OGENAAREKHUA

www.ingramcontent.com/pod-product-compliance
Lightning Source LLC
Chambersburg PA
CBHW072031080426
42733CB00010B/1854